*But what, my dear,
do you know about hotels?*

But what, my dear, do you know about hotels?

AND OTHER STORIES
ABOUT OLD TIMES IN COLORADO

By Florence Gellatly Means

Introduction by Nancy L. Widmann
Edited and annotated by Lorna C. Mason

GREENRIDGE PRESS

Means, Florence Gellatly, 1893–1973.
    But what, my dear, do you know about hotels? : and other stories
about old times in Colorado / by Florence Gellatly Means ;
introduction by Nancy L. Widmann ; edited and annotated by Lorna C.
Mason.
    p. cm.
    Includes index.
    ISBN 0-944720-02-1

    1. Colorado–History–1876–1950.   2. Colorado–Social life and
customs.   3. Women–Colorado–Biography.   1. Title.

F781.M43 1992   978.803'2'092
                                     QBI92-1021

Design: Diane Hoyt-Goldsmith
Production Management: Loreen Creative Services,
                        Wendy Staroba Loreen
Cartography: Reineck & Reineck

ISBN 0-944720-02-1

GREENRIDGE PRESS
5869 Greenridge Road
Castro Valley, CA 94552

To all those who are not native to
the San Luis Valley —
   Traditional English or Spanish rules of
   pronounciation do not work when
   naming "Saguache." It is a word of Ute
   Indian origin and pronounced
   "suh-WATCH."

*Saguache — that mispronounced, misspelled
name — where I was born.*

Marjorie Means Cogswell

FLORENCE GELLATLY MEANS

1893–1973

Preface

First of all, this book is an act of love. Florence Gellatly Means was my grandmother, and even to this day her gaiety, her charm, and her storytelling remain with me. I am the daughter of Marjorie, the eldest of her three daughters, and as the oldest grandchild was often called "the fourth daughter."

Florence Gellatly Means was always a wonderful story-teller. Those who knew her can hear in these stories the cadences and style of her oral storytelling. Not only are they entertaining stories, they present a way of life that has all but disappeared from modern America.

The majority of reminiscences were written by Florence Means in the last months of her life. In doing so, she was undoubtedly encouraged by the positive response to the private publication of her *Reflections of a Rancher's Wife* in December, 1972. Compiled by her daughter Laura Means Pope, *Reflections of a Rancher's Wife* was a collection of the columns she wrote from 1935 to 1937 for the Shepherdess Page of the *Colorado Wool Growers and Marketeer*. The

Gazette Telegraph of Colorado Springs praised *Reflections of a Rancher's Wife* for avoiding the "idyllical" and instead letting a picture emerge in the reader's mind of a "microcosm of life" in the West. Noting that "the length of a review does not depend upon the size of a book," the reviewer gave 44 inches of type to *Reflections*. Florence Means died less than a month after that review. Had she lived longer, there is no doubt we would have had more stories.

The story manuscripts, some typed and some handwritten, were found among family papers in 1990. In telling her stories, Florence Means had used pseudonyms for some names, for instance calling Herbert Hazard "Hubert Hilton." In the interest of history and the truth, real names have been substituted where possible for the fictional names. To this end, letters of the time, were particularly helpful. Also included in this collection of stories are three oral reminiscences that were taped about 1971.

Many have unstintingly helped with this project. Eileen Townsend did the initial word-processing. Without the generous nature of Diane Hoyt-Goldsmith, manuscript would never have become type. For his advice and support I thank my friend and colleague Malcolm Jensen. Frances Means Hoffman and Laura Means Pope were of immense help in providing background information. Eleanor M. Gehres, manager of the Western History Department of the Denver Public Library, made information from their files available to me and in addition put me in contact with Nancy L. Widmann, author of the Introduction. Finally I thank Margaret Finnerty, George Hazard, and Dean Coombs of Saguache as well as Jeanne M. Foster of Salida. By addressing my questions, large and small, they each have helped make this a better book.

Lorna Cogswell Mason

Contents

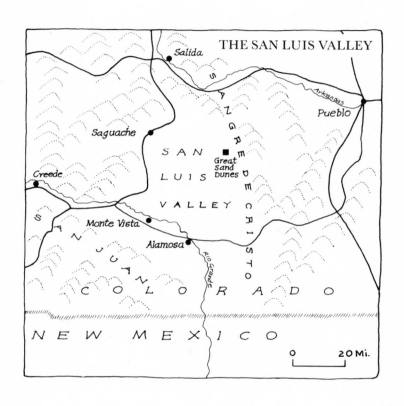

Introduction

Florence Gellatly Means, at almost eighty years of age, picked up her pen to write reminiscences. The result offers another valuable piece to add to our meager supply of first-hand truths from and about the lives of women during the Depression. Her motivations might have been only those of the natural storyteller, but while sketching the action in her personal history, she painted a 1930s Colorado landscape in feminine perspective.

The reader can enjoy Florence's reminiscences on many levels. First, she wrote her history in delightful story form. She made artful use of dialogue to advance her narrative, as though she closed her eyes and remembered word for word what was said so many years ago. The true characters and scenes in her 'stories' were described with understated wit and clarity. If only one could spend time at the 1935 Saguache Hotel listening to Florence play the piano and meeting the hotel guests — Sheriff Slim Paul who "looked a little like Will Rogers," the "pretty and gay" resident teachers who "were up to mischief, too, at times," and the dentist, Dr. Smith, whose "buzzer made static on the radio."

On a more serious historical level, the narratives affirm the importance of social status in the 1930s and the control that the desire for social status exerted, even in relatively remote small towns. Last, Florence's writing offers testimony to women's emerging search for adventure, economic independence, and participation as equals with men.

Women's diaries and reminiscences have the effect of placing the reader in the middle of a life story, without context, without a beginning and end. Women do not usually describe their geographic locales in historical detail, nor their actions in terms of unique accomplishment and conquest. Women living 'ordinary' lives write of the everyday details, the fabric of pragmatic decision making. By placing Florence Mean's story in context and then evaluating her details, the reader can touch a point of reality on the continuum of women's history.

The main story in the reminiscences is "But What, My Dear, Do You Know About Hotels?" which describes her experiences in running the Saguache Hotel. Florence is 43, living in 1935 Saguache, Colorado, on a large sheep ranch with husband Frank Means. The Saguache Hotel, a losing enterprise in disrepair, has fallen back into Frank's already debt-ridden world. Florence remembered how she bought the hotel for one dollar from her husband and turned it to profit despite a business naivete, lack of funds, and the prevailing view that women could not be taken seriously in business.

In the Afterword, Lorna C. Mason fills in the known details of her grandmother's successful foray into hotel management. She briefly highlights Florence's life after moving from Saguache and gives further evidence of Florence's insatiable need to find new challenges (like flying an airplane), always stretching the boundaries of the conventional woman's role. The reader is then treated to a bonus of five additional short 'stories.' They show off Florence Means' storytelling ability while confirming her inquisitive spirit. A Norman Rockwell quality pervades these glimpses of life on a home sheep ranch in a high mountain valley.

Saguache in 1935 was one of four major trading towns east of the San Juan Mountains in the partially irrigated San Luis Valley. Settled originally to support mining activities, agriculture, and livestock production, its function remained with the latter two after mining became less profitable. Sheep ranchers like Frank Means were able to use ancient transhumance shepherding techniques, with a home ranch for wintering the sheep and growing summer feed crops. Nearby mountain land supplied summer grazing and was either owned or leased from the government. Transhumance practices came from Iberia via Mexico with the first white settlers of southern Colorado, the Spaniards. Saguache has continued to reflect this heritage with its half Mexican-American population. The politically dominant Anglo population had settled from the east in the 1860s and the original population of Ute Indians had been removed to reservations in 1881. Saguache was still a small town in 1935 and remains so today with a population of about 600.

The Frank Means family would surely have been considered influential and of a high social status. Though the Depression forced Frank to struggle with mounting debt, he owned an automobile to drive the still dirt roads and dirt highways of their region. The automobile confirmed the family's connection to the larger Colorado community. As a sheep breeder, state legislator, and University of Colorado

Regent, Frank made frequent trips to the Denver area, 200 miles northeast. Florence drove as well, often alone to Boulder to visit her eldest daughter.

Between the lines of narrative, the reader feels Florence's struggle to maintain appearance and social status during the Depression. She, like others, sewed new clothes from the fabric of old clothes. She went without slips and new panties, but bought clothes for her college daughter Marjorie on credit. Florence and Frank stayed active in their local social clubs and church. Florence clearly placed great value on those associations and the camaraderie of women friends. She reflected an unconscious acceptance of the established social order and gave much energy to maintaining her position.

For all that conventionality, Florence had a keen awareness of the confusing conflicts surrounding male and female roles. At one point, she was denied a loan for a new hotel roof because she was a woman. "It was lucky I wasn't a man. What do they do when they have disappointments in business? At least I can cry."

Colorado women gained the vote in 1893, but the right had not given them any discernable political power or economic independence. By 1935, the hoopla over the 1920 national success of women's suffrage had long since been quieted by the insidious accusations of the Red Scare and the torment of the Depression. World War II had not yet encouraged women into the work force. If a woman worked it was because of desperate need at generally low paying, menial jobs. Florence Means augmented the family income by teaching piano, a socially acceptable pursuit for a woman with advanced education and middle class standing. A woman running a business was a rarity. Role models like Colorado's Josephine Roche, who ran her own coal mining business,

Rocky Mountain Fuel Company, with astute, progressive leadership, were far too few.

Where does Florence Gellatly Means fit on the continuum of women's history? For one view, it is helpful to step back and take a larger look at the experiences of Western women. In the nineteenth century Western Anglo women performed new tasks and tasted increased independence. Necessity of location forced this development. Women had to take on a variety of new responsibilities to establish homes and communities in a new environment. In the twentieth century, society continued to define women by gender, not by location, but this new dynamic learned through life experiences did not disappear. Despite societal pressures to keep the gender-based definition, women continued to expand their expectations. To add further complication, any notion of an expanded role for women was often working at odds with the rising importance of social status, fueled by increased immigration, labor unrest, and economic ups and downs. So, here is twentieth century Florence Means, a woman who clearly had the desire to maintain her social status, but who aspired to an expanding set of female expectations.

Florence Means was born the year Colorado women were enfranchised. Raised in Washington, she came to Colorado as a bride in 1913. She remained Frank's wife for a lifetime and her writing reflects a respect between them without indicating a close intimacy. Frank clearly made ranch decisions. That he left child rearing to her and gave her an allowance for all household and personal needs indicated his traditional control. Florence used that allowance — always too small in the Depression — as she pleased, augmenting it with piano lessons, later with hotel income, and banking it separately.

Florence found it necessary to consult Frank (a lawyer as well as a rancher) on major hotel decisions, yet she seemed to question her second-class status as Frank's wife. Though she was 43, she and Frank both thought she needed her father's approval to run the hotel. Florence evidently didn't get his approval, but went ahead without it. Florence's nature was to carry on despite obstacles. She found ways to succeed despite conventional biases against women in business — for instance, the automatic denial of credit to women without a male cosignatory. That she did this in a time of economic hardship makes it all the more remarkable. She found within herself an ability to hire and manage employees, to keep the books, to react well in a financial crisis, and to make good decisions.

It is interesting to note at times what is not included in Florence's reminiscences. At advanced age, Florence remembered how she had read the latest psychology to guide her in raising her two younger daughters. Yet, she does not mention her son who had died at age nine. Perhaps Florence as a storyteller felt her son's life was not germane to the story. Florence as a mother might have found it too painful. She also had few comments about the Mexican-American community. This was probably a true reflection of the lack of importance given any mingling of the two population groups at the time. Florence admired adobe architecture and at least one recipe in the Appendix is of Mexican derivation. Florence did not mention the women's political issues of the day. She might be amazed (or secretly pleased?) to be seen as one person who pushed against the accepted boundary of female role definition.

Florence was a woman who found untapped resources in midlife. Her abilities found an outlet in running the red brick

Saguache Hotel. Her lust for adventure, perhaps risk, was expressed in her meeting with the gypsies and in learning to fly a plane. But coexisting in Florence was the complex woman of her time who prized status and position, who was determined to maintain her social standing during the Depression, who wrote regular articles for the Shepherdess Page of the *Colorado Wool Growers and Marketeer*, who raised chickens first because everyone did, then out of need. Florence was the prototype of today's 'supermom' with her clubs, choir, and myriad social and family obligations overlaid with consuming business responsibilities. Her lighthearted writing style makes us picture a genteel lady, but when we consider the details of her narrative, set in context, a more complex picture emerges. History needs to tell the story of all the 'Florences.'

The historian's relatively recent recognition of the absence of a women's perspective has not found easy remedy. Diligent research has turned up some additional diaries and journals written by American women. Women do offer a separate perspective in any age. Yet women have sought anonymity as a natural component of their perceived supporting role in society. During the twentieth century, women have persevered less and less quietly, however, twisting and turning their way out of that role. Women did not burst forth into the business world as suddenly as it seemed in the 1980s. Their emergence has been a longer process and their story must be told.

There are not nearly enough writings by women to fill the void in women's history. It is a pleasure to introduce the writing of one woman, Florence Gellatly Means, because her reminiscences give a needed feminine perspective to life in the Depression for one woman rather determinedly twisting her way into a role of greater independence during difficult economic times, while still fulfilling her dutiful supportive role of daughter, wife, and mother. Thank you, Lorna Mason, for sharing your grandmother's reminiscences.

Nancy L. Widmann
Denver, Colorado

BUT WHAT, MY DEAR, DO YOU KNOW ABOUT HOTELS?

Foreword

Born in Philomath, Oregon, in 1893, Florence Gellatly grew up in Wenatchee, Washington. It was there she met the widower Frank Means. In the spring of 1910 Frank had married Bessie Carlberg of Wenatchee, but she died of typhoid fever a month after the wedding. Meanwhile, Florence had fallen in love with Norman Carlberg, Bessie's brother, but he was drowned in the Columbia River later the same summer. On subsequent visits to the Carlbergs, Frank began to woo Florence. After attending the University of Washington for two years, Florence married Frank Means in 1913.

Born in 1887 in Saguache, Colorado, Frank had received his law degree from the University of Colorado in 1907. He had practiced law for awhile in Idaho but had returned to Colorado after the death of his first wife. He made an effort to practice law in Saguache but found he preferred ranching. "I can't stand to listen another client's sad story," he told Florence. ("I thought I had married a young lawyer, but found his first love was sheep," Florence later said.) In 1914 Frank

2

was elected state senator in Colorado's Twentieth Assembly. His service in the Assembly apparently ended whatever law practice he had held. Yet Frank never completely gave up the law. He was always available to help friends and neighbors. Florence would get annoyed to hear someone say, "Frank, I just came by for some free advice." In 1921 Frank Means was elected to the Board of Regents of the University of Colorado, a position he held for sixteen years.

In the 1930s the Means' were land-poor. Poor prices, drought, and taxes had forced Frank Means to mortgage his 20,000 acres of ranchlands. (Of the Crash of '29, he would recall, "I went to bed one night with each sheep valued at $40 and, when I woke up, each one was worth $3.") During these years Florence Means supplemented the family's income by teaching piano lessons. Although she loved music, she really disliked the dreadful grind of so many lessons. And so she saw opportunity when her husband Frank found himself with an unwanted hotel. As she wrote her daughter Marjorie in April, 1935, "[Taking on the hotel] will be a good excuse to get rid of my music class. I'm so weary teaching, as I always am in the spring."

Like nearly every problem in life, one has to start with the tools at hand and not give up because of unalterable mistakes.

1 THE PROBLEM

It was a cold April morning in 1935. I sat shivering in the front seat of the car, waiting for Frank, my husband, to come out of the courthouse across the street. He had said he'd be gone just a minute, but it had already been twenty minutes. We were parked in front of the Saguache Hotel, and I should have stepped into the lobby to wait by the fireplace. I slid into the driver's seat to get the sun's rays through the glass and wriggled my toes to step up circulation. Springtime in the Rockies is surely not what the song by that name would lead one to believe.

As I sat waiting, I carefully appraised the hotel building from roof to foundation. It was soon to be ours again, or more accurately, Frank's. Colorado does not have community property. But his problems were mine too, and the hotel was definitely a problem.

Frank's father had built the hotel, to put Saguache on the map, as he had said.[1] He had been proud of the thirty-room brick structure and had hired people, usually a couple, to manage it. Upon his death, Frank had inherited it. Frank, a lawyer and rancher, with no interest in hotels, had promptly sold it to an uncle, Roll Means. Uncle Roll had done pretty well at first, but he could not have foreseen the Depression and had become more and more discouraged. He had finally decided to wait no longer for prosperity to round the corner and had given notice that he was leaving June first. So — the hotel would soon be ours again, back taxes and all.

To the casual observer, the hotel looked all right. Really better than all right. It looked good. It was the largest building in town except for the schools and the courthouse. It was substantially built and nicely proportioned. But to the close relatives, it gave a far different appearance. They knew, for instance, that it was built too low. It fairly nestled into the ground. The architect had evidently known nothing about "sub," which means that the water level is very near the surface of the ground. Consequently, when the neighbors flooded their lawns, the water rose higher and higher in the hotel furnace room and finally put out the fire in the furnace.[2]

Such mistakes are very fundamental. There was nothing to do at such times except explain to the freezing guests that you were doing everything that could be done, which, of course, was nothing. One couldn't bail water fast enough to keep the water level down because there was no place to bail

---

[1] Horace "Boss" Means (1855–1926) and a cousin, W.T. Ashley, had built the hotel in 1887, according to Jeanne M. Foster.

[2] Like other older communities in the semi-arid West, Saguache had (and still has) water ditches along the streets. Residents used this water to irrigate their lawns and gardens.

it to. It just sank into the ground and came back through the cement walls of the furnace room. Furnaces must be placed lower than the floor level of the building, it seems, to enable the hot water to circulate. That is a natural law of furnaces. So there were days in the spring when the hotel manager suffered utter exasperation while waiting for the local residents to stop irrigating. They were sympathetic, but could not be expected to go without lawns.

Another mistake, according to my way of thinking, was that the dining room did not face the street and the lovely courthouse yard across the street. That side of the building was cut up into rooms for the help. The dining room gave toward the alley on the other side of the building. The help had no time to enjoy the view, while the guests had no view to enjoy.

Dining guests gazed out upon the old Stockman's Club across the alley. It had been a saloon in the early days, was then domesticated into an ice cream parlor, and was now a plumbing shop and painted a colicky green. A lean-to back of the plumbing shop was painted white and from there a path led past the wood pile to an outdoor toilet. Not a very appetizing vista. This mistake was fundamental, too, because the central partition could not be moved without inviting the complete collapse of the building.

If nothing could be done about such things as the furnace and the dining room view, there were hundreds of things about which something could be done. Like nearly every problem in life, one has to start with the tools at hand and not give up because of unalterable mistakes.

In a few minutes Frank climbed in beside me and roared the car around the corner. He always roared the engine. Said it cleaned out the spark plugs. But I knew it was a trick he had learned when he had to crank the engine first and then race to reach the throttle before the engine died.

"What have you decided to do about the hotel, dear?"

"There's only one thing to do," he answered.

"You mean — ?"

"Nail up the windows."

"Surely you wouldn't do that?"

"Of course I would. I don't know anything about a hotel and I don't intend to learn."

"Why don't you lease it to someone?"

"I couldn't lease it the way it is. The whole thing is run down and worn out. They'd be calling me every ten minutes for new screen doors or new paint. You know, I have no time or money to put into that old place. If I come through without losing the ranches, I'll do well. I'm not going to chance losing everything we own to keep that hotel open."

"But we own the hotel, too. Perhaps someone would buy it."

"The only offer I've had was from Herbert.[3] He'll give me five thousand and the place cost thirty. I'll be damned if I'll give it away. I'll dismantle it first and sell the junk. You can never get a decent price for anything people know you don't want."

As we rattled over the stile into our ranch, I tried to visualize a perfectly bare spot where the hotel now stood. He couldn't really mean that kind of talk. But he might nail it up.

---

[3] George Herbert Hazard (1889–1949) was the assistant cashier of the Saguache County National Bank, according to George H. Hazard, Jr., Herbert's son. E.G. (Gordon) Gotthelf was the bank president; George Hazard, Herbert's father was the manager, and W.F. Boyd, the cashier. Nevertheless, Herbert Hazard was the one who most often dealt with the townspeople. Herbert's maternal grandmother, Flora Emma Means Stewart, was a sister of Horace Means.

The Saguache Hotel, built in 1887, had become a money-losing white elephant by the 1930s. Florence Means, however, saw opportunity, and with flair and persistence turned the hotel into a profitable venture.

"But what, my dear,
do you know about hotels?"

2 THE GLIMMER OF AN IDEA

The home ranch, like a great green carpet, lay almost level from the edge of the mesa to the mountains back of the town. It consisted of four hundred acres, mostly alfalfa, and was irrigated by water from the Saguache Creek. Saguache is an Indian word meaning "blue water," and the irrigation ditches, like tiny veins, literally gave life to the land.

Built at the edge of the mesa, our house faced the town instead of the ranch. It was elevated just enough to look over the top of the trees which shaded the town to the great San Luis Valley beyond. This valley had once been a lake, according to the Indians, and stretched level as a floor for over a hundred miles south. We had a fine view of Blanca Peak, the grandest of the Sangre de Cristo peaks, and on clear days we could distinguish the great domes at the end of the valley that were in New Mexico.

A small grove of trees protected our house from the west wind, and a tennis court[4] and pasture lay between it and the barns on the east. It is always well to have the barns and corrals away from the windward side.

I was always sorry that our house wasn't adobe, and it would have been had I known the history and background of the country. As it was, I had brought my [Pacific Northwest] environment with me — brown shingle bungalow. While we were engaged, Frank had written to ask whether I wanted a house of adobe or of wood. I in turn had written Frank and asked about adobe. To my query, "What is adobe?" his reply came back, "Adobe is mud." I made one more try: "Do nice people live in adobe houses?" He wrote, "I was born and raised in one." But that had in no way fired my imagination. If he had only explained that adobe is clay and straw made into neat bricks which after being baked in the sun make excellent building blocks, that neither heat of summer nor cold of winter can penetrate such a wall, and that the Mexicans who had them long before the white man came had found such houses especially suited to the climate and atmosphere of the place, it would have been different. Having been raised in an adobe house, he evidently had no idea how lumber in a very dry climate can shrink and shrink until the wind blows through every crack — especially around the fireplace and windows.

Our home was pleasant, I thought. Sometimes I regretted the dark oak paneling of which Frank was so proud, and the beams, which were only imitation and hung from the ceiling,

---

[4] In her reminiscences Marjorie Means wrote: "When I was older, Daddy built a tennis court for me. The only drawback was that it was dirt — not clay — and it took so much of my energy keeping the weeds off and rolling it smoothly, that I had little time to learn to play tennis."

so to speak, instead of holding it up. The fireplace though was pleasing, and we always had wonderful piñon wood for it. I had used nasturtium shades in the draperies to offset the heavy woodwork and had placed my most cherished possession, the piano, in the most conspicuous place, as *House Beautiful* had suggested. My Steinway piano was an upright — the room would not have accommodated a grand. Frank's father had given it to me as a wedding gift and was very proud that I played.

Josephine, my young Mexican maid, had the table set and was waiting to be told what to do. The population of Saguache was about half Mexican, and for very little one could hire a girl to come each morning to help with the dishes, cleaning, and ironing. On the whole, these girls were clean and willing and very good with children though very seldom assumed responsibility about cooking.

"Frances phoned that she's having lunch at Ruth's house, so I set only three places." Frances was seven and in the second grade. She was a year and a half younger than Laura Belle, so that some of the time they were seven and eight and some of the time seven and nine. I always had to stop and figure how old our children were. Laura Belle was only one year ahead in school because Frances had skipped the first grade, so they were almost like twins. We called our two young "the little girls" to distinguish them from our big girl, Marjorie, who was away at the university. A friend in Honolulu had called the young ones our ratoon crop. It seems that after sugar cane matures and is cut, a new little growth springs up called the ratoon crop.[5]

---

[5] The Means "ratoon crop" arrived after the sudden and unexpected death of their son Frank, age nine, in 1925.

The two little ones were very different in looks and temperament and seemed to complement each other. Laura Belle was dark and vivacious. Her eyes fairly danced. Frances was blonde, wide eyed, slower of speech and had a droll sense of humor, like her daddy. We called her our Will Rogers. I was trying to bring up these children according to the very newest ideas. The more psychology I read, the more convinced I was that Marjorie had grown to be a lovely girl in spite of me rather than because of anything I had contributed as her mother. Frank said that if the little girls turned out half as well as Marjorie, he'd subscribe to my ideas, but that personally he thought I treated the little ones as though I was their grandmother.

After lunch I walked out to the gate with Frank, the hotel still on my mind.

"It will be a real blow to this town if the hotel closes."

"Yes it will. That's why Roll has been hanging on. He says it will never open again if it closes."

"And what about court? This is the county seat. Where will the judge stay and who will feed the jury?"

"I don't know who'll feed them or where they'll stay. I'm not a philanthropist, and it isn't up to me to decide what they'll do."

"Well I think it is. That's your hotel and a property owner has responsibilities. I know you don't like owning it, but just the same those three thousand in back taxes are against your name, and it's up to us to do something about it."

"I am going to do something. Close it. I tell you it's a white elephant."

We both stood for a minute and then for no better response, I asked, voice wavering, "If I'd look after it, could I have it?"

Frank threw back his head and laughed. Then as he reached over to kiss me good-bye, he said, "If I thought you really wanted it, I'd make you a deed tomorrow. But what, my dear, do you know about hotels?"

"I've stayed in lots of nice ones," I countered.

With that he was gone. It was lambing season, a day-and-night job.

Frances and Laura Belle Means share a ride on one of Frank Means' Hampshire sheep.

*It was a whole new world—
undertaking something besides
piano lessons for profit.*

3 THE GROUND RULES

After Josephine had finished the dishes and was walking slowly down the hill, I opened the sewing machine in front of the dining room window, put a new stick on the fire, and turned on the radio. It would be two hours before the first music pupil came. One thing which the Depression had taught me was to sew. It was rather fun to rip up an old dress of Marjorie's, press the pieces flat, and lay out the pattern for something entirely new and different. The little girls wore anything of Marjorie's with delight because to them Marjorie and beauty were synonymous. I sewed slowly, carefully basting each part, and could never develop the abandon with which some people slash into things.

As I bent to my work, I mentally took over the hotel. It needed a sign in front — a tall neon sign which could be seen from the highway. The windows needed to be washed and a lattice fence built between the clothes lines and the front. But why enumerate all the things it needed? It was going to be closed down.

When a man works out of doors all day long, and the weather is cold and windy, the evening warmth of his home makes his face very red and tends to relax him completely. After dinner while I put the children to bed, Frank would read the paper. Often by the time I joined him on the other side of the fireplace, he would be sound asleep in his chair. He always said that he was only resting and knew everything that was going on around him, but his heavy breathing belied that claim. After his "forty winks" as he called them, he would rouse and enjoy the rest of the evening.

"I've been thinking of what you said today. You weren't really serious were you?" he asked me.

"Perhaps. I can't see why it would be any worse for me to close the hotel after I'd tried than for you to close it now."

"Where would you borrow the money?"

"From the bank. That's what banks are for, isn't it?"

"No — they wouldn't lend you the money. Besides they don't like it because I bank in Denver, so they wouldn't lend it to you as quickly as they would someone else."

"I'm not so sure about that. I bank here (thinking of my $124 a month) and besides they won't want to see the hotel closed. Every business will be hurt if you do that. I'd like to bet you that I can get the money. At least, it wouldn't hurt to try."

"Well, I'm not sure you want to undertake a thing like that anyway. You have your hands full with these children. Would you want to move down there?"

"No, indeed. A hotel is no place to bring up little girls. I'd have to get a good desk man and spend several hours a day there."

"Good desk men are hard to get. When you put your cash register in the hands of some at the salary you'll be able to pay, it just won't work."

"That depends."

"I don't think your father would like it either. He'd think I shouldn't let you do it."

"Maybe so, but I notice he did whatever needed doing, wherever he found himself. He can't say much."

"Well, you write him and get his reaction."[6]

In countering Frank's arguments I found myself in the position of defending something of which I wasn't fully sure myself — giving a service for which people would go out of their way to pay for, because certainly there weren't enough people in that town to assure its success.

"I guess I can make no decision until I find out whether or not I can get the money. That's the next step."

"That and writing your father. How much money would you ask for?"

"What do you think? Three thousand five hundred dollars?"

"That isn't enough unless I can get the commissioners to make some discount on the taxes. Roll wants a thousand dollars for the improvements he's put in there."

"I should have five hundred dollars anyway to start with besides the taxes and payment to Roll. I'll ask for three thousand five hundred and see what happens."

As we got up to go to bed, Frank said, "There are just two things I want you to remember. If you undertake this, I want you always to remember that I didn't ask you to do it, and I

---

[6] But her father, John A. Gellatly of Wenatchee Washington, did not approve. His attitude nearly nixed the whole project. (See the letter of Florence Means, April 27, 1935, on page 99.)

19

don't want you to talk about it at home. I couldn't bear to come home after a hard day's work to a delineation of the troubles at the hotel.

"That's all right. I'd rather make my own decisions anyway. But of course, you'll be my lawyer, won't you?"

"Oh I guess I'd have to do that. But honestly, I'd be happy if I never had to look at that hotel again."

"You'll never have to after it's mine. I promise."

The "home ranch," as the family called it, featured the wood bungalow Frank Means had built in 1913 for Florence, his bride. Florence, who was from the Pacific Northwest, later regretted that the house was not adobe, a building material she thought more suited to the climate of the San Luis Valley.

All I could do was try.
All I could do was try.

4 ASKING FOR MONEY

The mail came to Saguache twice a day. A little before noon the bus brought it from Alamosa some fifty miles to the south and around five in the evening from Salida, which was about the same distance to the north. Alamosa was on a branch of the Denver and Rio Grande between Pueblo and Creede. Salida was on the main line of the D & R G between Pueblo and Salt Lake so that mail from Denver or from over the nation could reach us by either route. Sometimes the passenger bus carried the mail, but usually it was the big freight bus. The driver would sound his horn as he turned off the highway into the town, upon which the postmaster would close the "window" and be standing at the side door while the big carrier backed up the sidewalk to disgorge sacks of mail and large amounts of parcel post.

Upon hearing the horn, all the families of the town would send someone to wait for the mail. They came from all directions, Mexicans and whites, and stood around the walls of the post office waiting until the postmaster distributed it. Some would gather in groups of two or three and visit and joke, while others stood in patient silence watching the movements of the postmaster through the little glass doors of the letter boxes. The boxes in the top rows were small and graduated to quite wide ones at the bottom. Ours was wide enough to hold a Montgomery Ward catalogue and often stayed unlocked for fear we might forget the combination and not be able to get our mail if the window were closed.

The evening mail was the most important to me because letters from the west came that way, via Salt Lake and Salida. All my family lived in the Northwest — brothers, sisters, aunts, uncles, cousins — besides my parents and girlhood friends. It had been very difficult for me to feel permanently located so far from all of them, and I constantly had the feeling of being a temporary resident of Colorado.

Our house was too far from Main Street to walk for the mail or even to hear the bus so we would jump into the car and hurry down — often for nothing but the ride.

I had made such a fruitless trip the day after our discussion about the hotel. Leaving the post office with only unimportant leaflets, I decided to drive slowly past the hotel, which was a block out of the way, and see how it looked in the evening. Smoke curled out of the chimney, and two cars were parked in front. One belonged to Slim Paul, the sheriff, who lived at the hotel. His license number was 1 in our county. The other car was from Denver. Well, at least they had one customer to stay all night, and it was still early.

As I turned the corner and started toward home, who should be crossing the street but Herbert; I started to drive on, then braked. It hadn't been definitely decided, and I hadn't written my father, but it would do no harm to feel him out.

24

"Herbert, may I speak with you a minute?" It wasn't so formal as at the bank.

"Surely, Florence. How have you been?"

"Fine, thanks. I guess you know, Herbert, that something has to be done about the hotel. Uncle Roll is giving it up, and Frank is going to close it the first of June. Do you suppose the bank would lend me some money if I took it over?"

"You mean, you, personally?"

"Yes."

"Would you move down there?"

"No, I don't feel that I should, on account of the little girls. But I'd get some good help at home and be there every day."

"What does Frank think about this?"

"Well he says he won't put a dime into it, so you must understand you're dealing entirely with me. But you know it would be a pretty hard blow to this town to lose the hotel."

"How much money would you need?"

"Enough to pay the back taxes and start. I'd like three thousand five hundred dollars. Frank will give me the hotel, you understand, taxes and all, but from there on I am on my own. I think I can do it, Herbert, if you'll back me." I was really talking myself into some self-confidence.

"Well, you understand that I will have to talk to the other men in the bank before I commit myself on a deal of this size. You must remember that the hotel business hasn't been too flourishing around here."

"I know it, but I'd like a try at it. You know they say prosperity is just around the corner."

I was so excited that I drove off in a cloud of dust without offering to take him home. One thing the hotel needed was a paved street from the highway to its front door. There was talk that the main highway from Salida to Alamosa was really to be paved at last. That would bring more tourists. But, of course the problem was to get them there. There was a lovely new hotel in Monte Vista thirty-six miles away, with a radio in every room. But at that there was a way — cheaper rates. Times were still very hard. A good comfortable bed, meals nicely prepared and served, for less money, would bring them. But how was this to be done at a profit? Fear slowly crept through my veins as I closed the garage doors for the night. All I could do was try. All I could do was try.

Frank Means poses with a prize ram. Although educated as a lawyer, Frank preferred raising purebred sheep.

It sometimes seemed that every time I looked out the window, something hungry was looking in.

5 MEANWHILE AT HOME

The smell of wool permeated the living room. Frank had not changed his clothes because he expected to go back to work after dinner. I never could figure out whether it was his shoes, his pants, or him that smelled so strongly of his business. Many times at night, after he had fallen asleep, I would get out of bed and put his clothes in the hall and open the windows wider. Ugh, that odor. And one time when I complained, he rubbed his hands together gleefully and said, "I have a confession to make. I *like* that smell."

And he did. He not only loved sheep, but he knew what looked good in a sheep. He could pick out a little lamb at a show which would grow into the finest ram in the country. Once he got fooled though when his choice began to grow very long legs. A tall sheep, it seems, has no charm for the sheep breeder. They must be compact and square across the back. But no matter what their shape, they all smell and have ticks. A tick crawling up your nightie when you reach for it to go to bed is not conducive to the best rest possible. Fortunately, sheep ticks don't bite people.

The nights were cold in May. Sometimes the days were, too, because our ranch was over 8,000 feet above the sea. Denver is known as the mile-high city, but we were a mile and a half high. This, of course, meant that our growing season was very short. Frost was apt to come until the tenth of June and usually killed my zinnias by the tenth of September. When the weather was very cold, as it was during the winter, we closed the fireplace because more warm air seemed to swoop up the chimney than the piñon fire could replace. But in the autumn, which is a glory of color in Colorado, and in the spring, the fireplace was a real joy. Our whole family life seemed to center around it.

The Mexican population burned piñon wood in their stoves almost entirely; when the barometer was low, the rich fragrance of it hovered over the town. It was so very heavy with pitch that one could start a fire with a match alone, but as a result it sooted up chimneys and burned out grates. Cedar was actually much better for a wood-burning cook stove and was just as fragrant in a clean sort of way. It was no good for the fireplace, however, as it popped onto the rug.

Our house was heated with a hot water furnace that burned coal. It held the warmth better than hot air but of course was dirty from the coal dust and ashes. We cooked with electricity and enjoyed the power for our iron, washing machine, and sweeper. Housekeeping on the ranch was probably no more complicated than in town except for the care of milk buckets, the churn, and whatever chores one assumed. These chores seemed to creep up on one. First someone would give the children a puppy, then Frank would give them a few pinko lambs.[7] I always managed to have some chickens, and the children's pony had to be taken back to the barn. It sometimes seemed that every time I looked out the window, something hungry was looking in. You got so your whole life hinged upon feeding things. Feeding the sheep, feeding the cows, the horses, the chickens, the dog, the children. But fortunately I never had to feed hired men. Since our property adjoined the city limits, our men went home for meals.[8]

We usually had our main meal at noon because, as Frank said, you couldn't work hard on a light lunch. This was better for me, too, because Josephine stayed just until the noon dishes were done, unless I was going to a party and needed her to stay with the children. Our evening meal was simple — sometimes leftovers from dinner or muffins and salad.

I decided not to mention my talk with Herbert because it had been a bit premature. Frank sat reading the *Wool Journal* and I knitted while we listened to the radio. I never could read while listening to the radio, but it never seemed to bother him.

"Would you like to walk over with me to make the rounds?" he asked.

"Surely, if you'll wait until I change my shoes." I slipped

---

[7] An orphan lamb, rejected by its mother and needing to be bottlefed.

[8] Frances Means Hoffman tells this story: When Mother was first married, she and Daddy went to sheep camp every year. Daddy always had a cook to feed the men, but one year in sheep camp the cook quit. Mother said, "Don't worry, dear, I'll cook for the men." So the first day she made a great big fruit salad. When the men came in, tired, they looked at it and grumbled and were very cross. So Daddy took her aside and said, "Now look, dear, the men are not used to having fruit salad for lunch. They want meat and potatoes and peas. So she said, "All right." The next day she got some steak. And it was very tough. So she decided to fool them and sharpen the knives so they wouldn't realize it was such tough steak. After the had served the steak and the potatoes and the peas, she looked up from the cooking area to see all the men eating the peas with their knives and cutting their tongues. After that Daddy sent her home, and she never cooked for hired men again.

into my short coat while he placed the screen in front of the fireplace.

It was very dark outside and the stars looked especially large and bright. It was always fun to find the Big Dipper and the North Star. Walking in the dark was uneven business on the road to the barn, so I always held tightly to Frank's hand or arm.

Frank slid back the bolt in the gate to the big corral, and we slipped through. Even in the dark one could distinguish the big dark pancakes which the cows had made, and I picked my way carefully while he went into the barn to turn on the lights. Instantly the place took on life — the soft bleating of the sheep in the pens and the rustle of the sheep herd as the large bunch in the main corral arose from their sleep and moved away from the gate. All the sheep in sight were expectant mothers, but the ones who were practically ready to drop their lambs were in the sheds lining the main corral on the north and west. These sheds were built that way so that the morning sun penetrated both shed and sheep and so that the wind, which was usually from the west, was kept out. These sheds were lighted with electricity and divided into small compartments which would accommodate from ten to twenty sheep. The sides facing the corral were built up with boards for about four feet, and canvas curtains rolled down to meet this board in case of a storm from the east or south.

Frank seemed to get the same thrill at finding new baby lambs as I did when gathering the eggs. I would lean over the open side of the shed while he walked through the herd.

"Well, well, is this big boy yours? Isn't he a beauty? Come now, Mama, and we'll find a more comfortable place for you two."

The sheep seemed really to love Frank, and the mother would stand by somewhat nervously while he lifted the baby by its two back feet. The mother would follow, baaing and lowering her head as if to catch the scent. They would cross the large corral amid all the sheep — poor lambie upside down, its mother close behind — and into the "hospital."

The hospital was a large canvas-covered building, which was divided into dozens of little pens about four feet square. Long aisles led through the building so that each separate pen opened into a runway. In the center of the building was a big iron stove. It looked like a huge black cat with short legs, its tail going up through the roof and its mouth big enough to accommodate huge chunks of green wood. The wood was piled to one side, and a couple of end-up nail kegs invited one to sit and get warm before going outside again.

Each pen had fresh, sweet-smelling straw bedding and a can or old bucket to drink from. It was a pleasant, warm building and I sat on a keg while Frank painted the new lamb's navel with iodine, brought a fork of sweet alfalfa, and left mama to lick her baby clean and dry. Next morning he would come by to see if 'Junior' had nursed.

It must not be imagined that all sheep men had such elaborate improvements for lambing as Frank did. Many of the large herds lamb right out in the open. But Frank raised purebred and registered sheep for breeding purposes. They were more valuable as individuals, they had to be carefully watched so that the papers of registration were correct, and it was better to lamb as early in the year as possible so that they would be large enough to sell by fall. Frank's sheep were Hampshires. They had black legs and faces and no horns. They were largely raised for meat and did not have the long fine wool, for instance, of a Rambouillet.

I must feel free to institute all sorts of innovations.

6 MAKING PLANS

It would require at least seven people to staff the hotel — a front man, a cook, janitor, chamber maid, dishwasher and two waitresses. The man at the desk or front man seemed most important. He would make decisions in my absence, greet the guests and thus create the atmosphere of the hostelry, must manage the help and must be honest, keep the books and be able to type menus, etcetera. In addition to these intellectual and managerial abilities, he must be able to make a good Coke. Such a combination seemed fantastic. Many boys who were pleasant and smart weren't careful about the cash register. Often those who were honest were too stupid. It would seem that anyone who had the attributes I expected would be operating his own business at a huge profit instead of working for his room and board and fifty dollars a month. That was all I felt I'd be able to pay.

I thought and thought and evaluated everyone I knew but finally came up with exactly the right person. I am convinced that for every combination of requirements there is someplace an available person with exactly such attributes. Donald Polson was the nephew of a dear friend of mine. He had contracted tuberculosis while attending Annapolis and had spent six long years at Fitzsimmons Oaks Hospital. Frank and I had often driven out to see him and had grieved to see such a fine mind and sensitive personality wasting away. He had made a brave fight and had worked on the newspaper in between relapses. He might be able to undertake some work where he was his own boss. I wrote and asked if he would consider such a position. If he could get a bill of health to work in a public place, the rest of it could be worked out I was sure.

Donald was delighted at such an idea. He had taken it up with the Colonel, he wrote, and would let me know what the report showed. He was eager for a change, wanted to stay in Colorado, would get compensation, and thought such an experience would be most interesting.

I waited eagerly for his final reply because I knew he would be able to help make decisions about many things. I wrote him that things weren't settled yet but that I was seriously considering taking over the hotel.

Next in importance to the front man, was the cook. The cook who was at the hotel, Bessie Woods, was excellent.[9] She and her sisters had done most of the work there for years. But I knew that I must let them go. I was unexperienced and they knew it. They would have no faith in all my new ideas and would tend to carry on as usual. The hotel hadn't succeeded so I must feel free to institute all sorts of innovations. It would be difficult to make the Woods girls understand that I had

[9] This was probably a fictitious name. In her letters at the time Florence Means made reference to the "Burch girls."

nothing against them. Perhaps one of them could help me at home. I needed dependable help there. Then they would know that there was nothing personal in their dismissal.

For the housekeeper or chamber maid and the janitor a couple would be ideal. My janitor must be a painter, a plumber, an electrician and general fixit man. The last word, fixit, rang a bell. A nice looking couple had recently moved to town from the dust bowl area and had hung out a sign "The Fixit Shoppe." Everyone laughed about the "Shoppe" and called it the Fixit Shoppie. Frills are rather ridiculed in small western towns. But I didn't react that way. Evidently they wanted their shop to be a little extra special.

One evening on the way home from town I walked by the Fixit Shoppe to meet Mr. and Mrs. Cummings and asked if they would consider moving into the hotel (if I took it over). I explained that the salary wouldn't be large, but they'd have a warm room and all their meals — no overhead at all in fact. Mr. Cummings was a tall angular man who could do upholstering, painting, carpentry, etcetera. He had a dignified manner and a philosophical way of speaking. His wife was pretty, had naturally curly hair, and, I noticed, kept her windows sparkling and the rough-finished room very neat and clean. If she was strong enough, she would manage nicely, I was sure.

The exodus of material from my house to the hotel had begun.

7 TAKING CHARGE

I found it very difficult to realize that the hotel belonged to me. Just signing a paper seemed such a little thing to assume ownership of the place.[10] When expecting a baby for instance, one plans and dreams for weeks before taking responsibility and is psychologically and emotionally prepared when the baby arrives. But to walk across a familiar threshold and suddenly realize that the dirty windows reflected upon *me* as a housekeeper was quite a shock.

"Donald, don't you think we should wash the windows inside and out, first of all?"

He evidently hadn't noticed them, for he said, "Come here," and walked behind the fountain.

Trained as he was in a tubercular hospital, he was quick to see a hiding place for germs. It seemed that the fountain, which looked like any other from the front, was merely a

---

[10] Frank Means had sold Florence the hotel for one dollar.

sham. There was no drainage at all. The water drained into buckets which had to be carried out the back.

"I won't serve people from a place like this," he said. "Even the water for washing the glasses has to be carried in and out, and you know it isn't sanitary. There is no way to keep hot water here."

I could see that the fountain needed attention. Discarded straws and paper cups stuck out of dirty buckets, but as I stood puzzling, Mrs. Cummings leaned over the top rail of the stairway to say, "There are two whole sheets in the linen closet. With what shall I make up the beds?"

How had they managed? Evidently washed the ones on the beds and put them back the same day. Fortunately it was June. January might not permit of such speed.

"Put those two on, and I'll bring some from home until we can order new ones. Have you a Montgomery Ward catalogue, Donald? I'll bring mine down."

I walked on through the dining room. A row of dark booths with sagging heavy dark red curtains lined one side of it. Neither the partitions between the booths nor the curtains came within two feet of the floor. Inside each enclosure was a square table and four chairs. I suppose one was supposed to feel very private and exclusive inside such a place or free to eat with one's knife, but I always felt caged in. I like people and wanted to know who else was eating at the hotel. It is pleasant to see friends and an interesting diversion to see strangers in such a small town. Once in a while a strange dog would appear under the partition and beg for your steak bone, but other than getting a thrill from eating out, you sat and looked at your own family, as at home.

On the other side of the long dining room extended a counter with a refrigerated showcase now full of meat. The idea was to walk past the meat, select what you'd care to eat, take a stool, and watch it cooked before your eyes on a grill just behind the counter. The grill was greasy black and had a tin background which completely covered one of the windows. The other windows, which were all behind the counter, too, looked out upon the alley and the tin-roofed, unpainted building beyond.

A large chrome coffee urn stood on one side of the grill and a shelf of Campbell's soup on the other. This must all be changed, I thought. This dungeon of a dining room was noted for its good steaks, french fries, and hot biscuits, but it must take a sturdy digester to enjoy eating even those good things in such a place.

Pushing the swing door into the kitchen, Esther Anderson, the cook, had that frustrated look of one who agrees to work for someone she never sees.

"What shall we cook today?"

"Make some pies, Esther. Boil some potatoes which can be fried upon order, open some peas, and depend upon short orders for a day or two. Sunday we'll really knock 'em cold with a super menu.[11] While you're waiting for customers, you could clean that stove inside and out. We're going to do our cooking back here. And the storeroom shelves need clean papers. The J.S. Brown man should be here tomorrow to take our order. Make a note of what you think we need. Have you some lettuce and tomatoes to make a salad? Try making a perfection salad for tomorrow.[12] Cabbage is cheap and a gelatine salad keeps a

---

[11] According to Laura Belle Means Pope, Florence Means served up a Sunday dinner as if she were serving guests in her own home. The menu that first Sunday included roast leg of lamb with browned potatoes, peas, salad, and a variety of pies. Only two guests showed up for dinner, much to Florence's disappointment.

[12] Florence Means' recipe for perfection salad is in the Appendix.

couple of days. You can always use ice cream from the fountain for ala mode pie, or alone, if they don't care for pie. I'll have Donald type the menus."

I stepped from huge kitchen onto the back porch, which gave to the furnace room as well as to the sheds on the back of the lot. There was just room between the sheds and hotel proper for a truck to drive through from the main street to the alley or vice versa. The Valley Packing Company brought quarters of meat here twice a week. The transportation company delivered cases of groceries, and the coal truck noisily unloaded its bumpy cargo down a metal chute. The ashes, too, came out here and now, having filled up the ash pit, were piled in unsightly mounds of gray waste toward the street. These had to be hauled away by someone — but it was almost noon and I had little folk coming home for lunch. All I had accomplished, it seemed, was to walk in one end of the hotel and out the other. Nothing was really done.

After lunch I drove up to the curb with a Montgomery Ward catalogue, a dozen percale sheets and pillow cases, and my wall brush. The exodus of material from my house to the hotel had begun. Someday, I vowed, the take would go the other way.

Donald was still worrying about the fountain. I could see he'd get nothing done until that matter was corrected.

"I called Denver a few minutes ago and find we can get a used Bishop and Babcock Fountain for eight hundred dollars. Having it installed would cost another two, so I think that for a thousand dollars we can really make this a beautiful lobby. My idea is to set the fountain back along the west wall and then build an L shaped extension for the registration desk. That way one person can mix and serve drinks, register guests, operate the cash register for the dining room, and sell magazines."

"Sell magazines?"

"Yes, they're bright and attractive and don't cost anything. All you have to do is be sure the covers are torn off and returned for credit when they don't sell. It takes a little postage but makes the place look up-and-coming. I could picture Donald, surrounded by his beloved magazines. It was a correct background for his thoughtful manner. Coca Cola signs and posters usually suffice for a front man but not when Donald was in charge.

"Do you think we need a fountain? I can't think of any other hotel which has one."

"Certainly — someone has to stay here all day anyway, and he might as well sell enough to help pay his salary. We can sell candy bars, Planters Peanuts, razor blades, cigarettes, cigars, and you know, a Coke or milk shake to people who drop in. We're right across the street from the picture show and that makes this an ideal fountain spot."

It sounded reasonable. Uncle Roll had said, "Keep the lobby bright, encourage people to come in by the fireplace, and, while they're visiting and standing around, some of them will spend a nickel. Always be glad to give the children a drink of water when they come in after school because they'll see someone go out with an ice cream cone and you know — it forms habits for spending in the right place."

I hated to ask for more money. A thousand extra seemed a great deal when I already owed Herbert three thousand. But it wouldn't hurt to ask. Then if I was refused, Donald would have to think about something else.

Herbert and I went into the back room. I explained about the buckets — the unsanitary arrangement, the place for a new desk, the magazines, and he agreed. Yes, he would forward a thousand more. But I had the feeling that this was not to become a habit. He wasn't entirely surprised by my fancy ideas but couldn't forget my lack of business experience. He gave it to me with a sort of 'let this be the last time' pat. I was sure it would be.

Milo Means, a cousin of Frank Means, stands behind the lobby fountain of the Saguache Hotel in a photo taken before Florence took over the "white elephant." (Photo courtesy of Milo Means)

Only one thing upset us about teachers. They didn't eat anything.

8 THE GUESTS

When managing a small town hotel in a state like Colorado, it is well to have a number of permanent guests. It is a long cold stretch between tourists. During that time the coal bill assumes exaggerated proportions, and the light bills make a sharp curve upward. And there is always the chance cold-blooded guests will use electric heaters in their rooms.

There were six resident guests living in the hotel when I took it over. Some school teachers, the local druggist, and the sheriff. They were all very dependable people and paid their bills promptly on the first. With this backlog of patronage and with very little additional income, one could just barely keep going during the winter.

The rooms in the Saguache Hotel were all outside rooms with a long hall extending from the front stairs to the back of the hotel, where the public bath rooms, ladies toilet, and back stairs were located. The upstairs plan looked a little like a strip of bacon with a wide side and a narrow fat side and the lean hall running between them. The outside rooms were much larger than the inside ones and looked out upon the lawn, the tree-lined street, and the courthouse yard across the street. The smaller inside rooms gave toward the alley and the unpainted building beyond.

All the rooms rented for fifteen dollars a month, inside or out, so naturally everyone had an outside room. Donald and I talked this situation over and decided that the regulars should have the inside rooms. The teachers were at school all day anyway and shouldn't mind the lack of view. Then the outside rooms would be free for transients. I could recall that, when I went to Denver with Frank on business trips, I always enjoyed watching from my hotel window. Even fire engines are exciting, not that Saguache had one. It would surely be deadly to sit all day in one of our inside rooms. So we hit upon a plan. After September first the outside rooms would be eighteen dollars a month, and the inside, fifteen dollars as usual. Everyone moved but one teacher. She liked her room and didn't mind the three dollars extra.

It was a great asset having the teachers in the hotel. They were pretty and gay, and some of them could play the piano. Only one thing upset us about teachers. They didn't eat anything. I'd never try to make a living boarding teachers. Of course, they were watching their figures, and I was in no position to belittle that. Try as I would, I never could find any food which disagreed with me. The teachers would have just coffee for breakfast. We had to put on the menu that for orders less than twenty cents, each cup of coffee would be five cents.

The girls were up to mischief, too, at times. They discovered someway that by moving the clock on the stair landing just a tiny bit, they could stop it. Methodical Donald was quite distraught trying to keep the time of day but never actually saw anyone touch the clock.

On the whole, however, I felt that the teachers added much charm and warmth to the hotel. They were pretty and pleasant and complained very little. I loved them all.

Slim Paul, the sheriff, was a great asset, too. It was just like having a house detective, only instead of paying him, he paid me. He was tall and thin and looked a little like Will Rogers. He noticed every car license which parked in front of the hotel and had the local population evaluated accurately. He was a man of few words unless you got him started about his M.P. days in the army.[13]

When the sheriffs' state convention was held in Glenwood Springs, Slim brought home a beautiful bronze trophy. He was, it seemed, the best shot of any sheriff in Colorado. He put the trophy on the mantelpiece, and I worried when I saw it still there at eleven o'clock that night. The hotel door was always left unlocked. Since anyone could simply walk in and walk out with the trophy, I hesitated about hiding it in the

---

[13] Edward Ivan "Slim" Paul (1891–1960) was legendary for his ability to catch criminals. He was a cowboy before serving as a military policeman in World War I. After the war, Saguache cattlemen looking to end the widespread rustling elected Slim Paul as sheriff. "It turned out," he later said, "the rustlers were some of the same people who backed me for sheriff." Recalled a Saguache merchant: "Slim was never shot at much, though he handled some of the ornerist desperados in the country. They knew if they missed they'd be deader'n hell a couple of seconds later." Slim actually never shot a man. In fact, according to a former assistant district attorney, "He just sent word to the suspect, often by a sheepherder, and the man usually came in on his own accord." ("Empire Magazine," *Denver Post*, May 21, 1950)

In 1940 Slim married Sara "Sally" Thacker, an English teacher in Saguache who had also stayed in the hotel. In 1943 Slim again went to war, serving with both infantry and armored divisions in Europe. On his return he became Brand Commissioner of Colorado, and he and his wife lived in Denver. Slim is buried in Saguache.

desk. Finally I decided it would take a lot of nerve for anyone to steal from the best shot in the state. I turned the lights low, put a few keys of available rooms beside the register, and left.

The druggist had a room downstairs that he had occupied since the hotel was first built. I knew he was the only one in the house who could really compare my management with those before me. Someday I would ask him how we were doing. We had no basis of comparison.

Early in the fall we had a letter from a young dentist, Dr. Smith. He was locating in Saguache. He would like to rent two rooms — one for his office and one for a reception room. He thought perhaps we could put a cot in his reception room so that he could use it for a bedroom at night. It entailed some plumbing to equip the office, but we were delighted to rent two rooms on the main floor in the annex. We made him a rate of twenty-five dollars a month for the two. Of course, he would eat his meals there, and all his patients would have to walk past the fountain going in and out. They just might feel like treating themselves to an ice cream soda after having a tooth extracted!

There was only one complaint about the dentist. His buzzer made static in the radio. You couldn't hear a thing while it was on. The hotel radio was on top of the piano in the lobby, and it had wonderful reception. On Saturday afternoons during the football season, all the men from the courthouse would gather in the lobby to hear one broadcast. Donald would build a big fire in the fireplace, and eight or ten men would sit listening and smoking. One afternoon I walked in just as C.U. [Colorado University] was making a first down and to my utter amazement saw one of Dr. Smith's patients sitting on the piano stool with a white napkin pinned around his neck. Dr. Smith, instrument in hand, was leaning against the wall. The only time he could grind was between quarters or during time out.

Then one more teacher moved in so that by year's end we had eight permanent guests, one of them using two rooms. The help all lived in the hotel, too, so that with no extras, fifteen people slept there each night. We began to wonder how many permanents we dare take. We certainly didn't want to run short of transient rooms in case there should be a sudden spurt of business.

Slim Paul, center, meets old friends E. B. Noland, left, and G. H. Curtis, right, in front of the Saguache Hotel in 1950. By that time the famous sheriff had become Brand Commissioner of Colorado. (The Denver Post)

"Did you know that the plaster fell off on a lady in bed yesterday?"

9 A LEAKING ROOF

Ranchers in the San Luis Valley usually start haying in July, right after the Fourth. Unfortunately, that is when the rainy season also starts. The mornings dawn clear and bright but by two o'clock in the afternoon, severe storms may burst upon the working hay crews. The natives say that if, in the morning, you see a fluffy little cloud just peeking over the top of Devil's Knob mountain, you may expect rain by afternoon. Oddly enough, this seems to hold true. That innocent little cherub grows into a towering white cumulus giant who advances steadily across the valley, rumbling, bumping, and pounding the atmosphere as he goes. He hurled crooked shafts of lightning at trees, rocks, and telephone poles. It is quite terrifying. I've often wondered if war sounded like that.

Many people are afraid to use the telephone or stand in a doorway during such electrical storms, and some suggest sitting on a bed. Frank always took out his watch and counted the seconds between the lightning flash and the ensuing clap of thunder. He could thus determine the distance to the unfortunate spot which received the bolt. I presume, by his method of deduction, you'd know you were struck, if the two came exactly together. Horses were supposed to attract lightning, and cowboys wisely dismounted and stood some distance from their ponies during a storm — so I was told.

Having grown up in the Northwest where steady drizzles gently lull one to sleep at night, I could never feel exactly comfortable during these mountain storms. The rain lashed the window panes and blew into the screened porch to wet the rug and couch covers. It seemed to be hurled from buckets. The chickens ran for cover with drooping, dripping tails, and stupid young turkeys would just lie down and die if one didn't rescue them. The accompanying wind broke limbs from the trees, and my delphinium would be twisted and broken.

It was over as quickly as it came. The sun came out as though nothing had happened. But the hay was wet, and the horses had to be unhooked from the mowing machines and rakes. They came past the house in their clanking harnesses on the way to the barn. Then it was quite a task to think up enough jobs to keep the hay crew busy for the rest of the day. At such times I had help in the yard or even got the chicken house cleaned.

After one particularly bad storm I splashed down to the hotel. Upon entering the front door I could detect the unmistakable smell of wet plaster. I glanced at the lobby ceiling but could detect no damage. Walking through to the kitchen, I found Mr. Cummings collecting empty fruit and coffee cans.

"I hate to mention it," he said, "but something must be done about our roof."

"What's the trouble?"

"It leaks like a screen."

Esther was peeling boiled potatoes. "Did you know that the plaster fell off on a lady in bed yesterday?" she asked. "In Number 8."

"Heavens! I might be sued. I could smell it when I came in. Where does it seem to be the worst?" I asked.

"All over," said Mr. Cummings. "I climbed up into the attic and put cans around wherever it seemed to be the worst, but they fill up and run over. Then too, one of the attic windows is broke and when the rain comes from the south it wets the ceiling of Number 11."

"You can fix that, can't you?" I asked.

"Yes, but if this rain keeps up, the whole second floor will be ruined. The only part which is any good is the annex. It's newer. I don't think this roof has been oiled or painted for years."

"How much would a new roof cost?"

"I'm not sure but my guess is it could be done for two or three hundred dollars. You can buy rolls of that asphalt tiling and put it on right over the shingles. That would be cheaper than a new roof and even better."

As I drove home my spirits were as dampened as the landscape. I simply couldn't ask Herbert for any more money. There seemed to be no end to the needs of that hotel.

All evening I kept thinking about roofs. Roofs — Johns-Manville. Those words were synonymous. They were a big company and must have offices in Denver. They surely were eager for business, and I was eager for a roof. If they would only trust me to pay something each month, it could be done. I had a friend who worked for that company in Seattle, and he said they were very nice.

The next morning I wrote a letter to Johns-Manville Company, Denver. I explained my need and asked their advice about the proper roofing. Their answer was back in three days. They, it seemed, would be delighted to furnish me with a roof. They favored composition roofing for a job like mine and could deliver upon receipt of my order. They would be happy to accommodate me with monthly terms, but would, of course, expect the signature of the mortgagee.

The mortgagee. Who was he? They must mean Herbert.

I had promised not to talk about the hotel at home, but sometimes I just had to ask a few questions. "Dear, what is a mortgagee?"

"A mortgagee? Why, the man who holds a mortgage on a given property."

"Is Herbert my mortgagee?"

"Yes, why?"

"Well, I wrote to Johns-Manville about buying a new roof on the installment plan, and they say they must have the signature of the mortgagee. Why, I wonder?"

"Simply because the roof is going onto his building. That is, if you fail and he takes the hotel, he'll have the roof and will have no obligation to pay for it, unless they have his signature."

"I wouldn't think he'd mind signing something like that, would you? It would be his roof."

"Depends upon how deep he cares to go into this thing. He's already put up a good deal, don't you think? He no doubt figures that the more you owe, the harder it will be for you to pay out."

I said no more but wondered how one could be expected to pay out when plaster was falling on the guests. We simply had to have a roof. There was no way but to speak to Herbert.

I walked into the bank and asked to speak to him privately. We went into the back room, and I explained it all. Finally I told him about the mortgagee's signature. "You see, Herbert, I'm not asking you for any money, just your signature. If I fail, you'll have the hotel and you'd need a roof the same as I do." It sounded convincing to me.

Herbert sat a moment, saying nothing. He was a good friend of mine. I taught his children piano lessons and respected him for his love of music. He looked at me kindly and in a quiet voice said, "Florence, I can't see my way clear to put any more into the hotel. I hate to refuse you, but I must."

It was as simple as that. Perhaps he didn't have any more money. Or perhaps he was afraid that I'd give up. At least it was final. I must somehow buy a roof on an installment plan that didn't require the mortgagee's signature.

Ping pong, pong ping, the drops of rain fell into coffee cans, and the wettest season in years dragged on. Room after room showed ceiling spots, and the damp smell of plaster greeted the guests. But quite a few people stopped at the hotel anyway. Cochetopa Pass was slick and dangerous when it was wet, and many tourists decided to stay overnight and take the pass in the morning when the sun was shining. So the rain had some advantages. One car from Texas took three rooms, and the guests all ordered T-bone steaks for dinner. They didn't seem to notice the plaster.

When I turned on the radio after dinner one night, a government man was talking. He said that you could rebuild your farm building or town property by borrowing from the government. That was an idea. "Paint up, repair your barn, fix your roof" — he seemed to be talking to me. He even gave the names of people to contact and the one for our county was a Mr. Clark in Salida. I knew of him. He was a lumber man and evidently prepared to sell the materials and furnish the credit under this plan.

So, I wrote another letter describing my needs to the government representative. At the end of the letter, I explained about the mortgagee. "If you must have the signature of the mortgagee to make this loan, please do not go any further, because that I cannot get."

A nice reply came from Salida. The government representative would be in the valley within a few days and would call upon us personally to make the necessary arrangements. He would make an estimate of the material required and rush the matter to a conclusion as they could clearly appreciate my need. They would not require the signature of the mortgagee.

Wonderful. Evidently one could succeed if determined enough. Mr. Clark arrived about ten o'clock one morning and we showed him all the damage. Mr. Cummings went with us and I thought talked too much, but he knew more about measurements, costs, freight, etcetera, than I did, and, after all, he was the one who had to put on the roof.

We ended up in the lobby. Donald mixed a Coke for each of us, and we sat around the white porcelain-topped ice cream table while Mr. Clark made out the necessary forms. The government, it seems, always has forms. He filled in all the spaces, complimented me upon my undertaking, saying he saw a real future for the hotel business in Saguache. At last I picked up the pen and signed Florence G. Means — Owner. But under my name was another dotted line followed by Mortgagee.

"But, Mr. Clark, I wrote you not to come if you had to have the name of the mortgagee." A great lump was coming into my throat.

"Well, surely the mortgagee cannot object to signing this. It makes the property more valuable. The roof will be his if he should foreclose."

"But he doesn't want a roof. Just I want a roof," I explained. "I told you specifically not to expect his signature."

"Well, well, Mrs. Means, I'm surely sorry." He gathered up his papers and put them into his briefcase. "Why don't you take the matter up again with Mr. Hazard? I really can't see how he can have any objection."

"But he does." That's all I could think of to say.

Mr. Clark, after taking hours of our time, drove away. I stood a minute not knowing what to say to Donald and Mr. Cummings and then turned, went up stairs, walked the full length of the hall to the ladies' rest room, sat down on the toilet, and cried. It was lucky I wasn't a man. What do they do when they have disappointments in business? At least a woman can cry.

"You know, Mrs. Means, you can buy roofing at Monkey Wards on the installment plan."

10 DRY AT LAST

Mushrooms were springing up in our backyard, so I knew it wasn't my imagination that this was an unusually wet season. (I was always a little nervous about eating mushrooms, but Frank said if they were pink underneath, they were perfectly safe. He'd even eat puff balls and so far had suffered no ill effects.)

Still it rained everyday and sometimes at night. You'd think that so much moisture would swell up the shingles and stop up the holes, but it didn't seem to work that way. It must just have washed out all the dust caulking and cleared the way to the holes.

The hotel staff ate their meals in the kitchen, and I knew that at such times they discussed the guests, the local gossip, my problems, and my chances for success. They were loyal and on the whole, a high-class bunch. The fact that I had to ask their advice about so many things made them seem more like partners than helpers. As I walked into the kitchen one day,

Mr. Cummings was pouring over a Montgomery Ward catalogue.

"You know, Mrs. Means, you can buy roofing at Monkey Wards on the installment plan."

"You can?" I wondered why I hadn't thought of them.

"Yea, I figured out the yardage, and it will cost $248.17 to cover the main part of the building. I can lay it right over the present roof, and it will make a sort of insulation. What color would you like?"

I looked at the picture and description. There it was: "colorful, durable, economical, provides long-wearing, fire-resistant protection for farm buildings, homes, workshops, sheds," and it should say hotels. "Nails needed for applying, lap cement and complete instructions are included for applying over old roof covering, order the roofing packed with 1-1/2 inch nails. In tile red or forest green." Since the hotel was red brick, forest green would surely look better. The reds might clash. "For full information regarding Ward's Monthly Payment plan, see inside back cover," etcetera, etcetera.

The back of the catalogue had several pages with order blanks on one side of them. I tore one out, and we checked and rechecked the amount needed, and I ordered the new roof. For some reason, it hadn't occurred to me that mail order houses would carry supplies of this kind.

I had a prompt and courteous reply from Montgomery Ward saying they would be happy to ship my roof but that for orders of over one hundred dollars they must have the signature of my husband. That should be easy I thought.

But it wasn't.

Frank came in late for dinner. He had gone to Center on business, and so the children and I had already eaten when he drove in. I brought his supper from the oven and sat down opposite him, to visit while he ate.

"Well, dear, it looks as though we're going to have a new roof on the hotel after all."

"Good," he said.

"Montgomery Ward says they will be glad to send it to me, but that for orders over a hundred dollars they must have your signature. Could you just sign your name here?" I had everything ready, even the pen.

"But I told you I wouldn't put anything into the hotel."

"I'm not asking you for anything. This is just a formality."

"Just a formality — where did you get that idea? It's a liability, and I told you when you took the hotel, to count me out. No, I won't sign it."

"I can't see why. I sign those old papers you send to the bank." I sensed injustice.

"I'll tell you why. I'm in debt. I borrow money from the bank. And every year I make a list of my assets and my liabilities in what is called a bank statement. You can surely see, can't you, that it doesn't help my credit any to be buying something at Montgomery Wards for ten dollars down and ten dollars a month."

"Would you have to put it down?" I asked.

"Certainly I'd have to put it down if I signed my name to that order. No, I can't sign it. That's why I asked you not to trouble me about the hotel."

The next day Mr. Cummings and I talked it over. I think all the staff thought I had a very hard-hearted husband. Even the girls in the dinner club thought so. Frank and I went to dinner club at his cousins the next night, and I told them what a time I was having and that even my own husband had turned me down.

"Why I'd choke him," said Betty.

All the husbands loudly sympathized with me for having such a husband. I could see they thought it a huge joke. No one seemed to take my business venture seriously.

It still rained. The roof had become an obsession with me. I'd make one more try. I composed a letter to the manager of Montgomery Ward and marked it Personal. No secretary must throw this into the waste basket. I explained my troubles in full — the constant rain, the plaster falling on the lady in bed, the mortgagee, the government, and now my husband's signature, which I could not get. I explained that the hotel was mine — all mine — and that I always paid my bills, that I was an honest person. He could call up Daniels and Fisher or the Denver Dry Goods where I had charge accounts and find out if that was not true. I made a final appeal. I simply had to have that roof, and I could guarantee they would never regret selling it to me. Sincerely, Florence G. Means.

That evening I told Frank about the letter. "That sounds okay," he said, "only you should never have told them that you were honest. Whenever you do that, they immediately suspect that you aren't." I sometimes suspected Frank of enjoying my troubles, but it was too late to change the honest part now.

In three days I received a reply to my plea. I nervously tore open the envelope. It read, "Dear Madam: We note with interest the difficulties you are having with your hotel and are happy to report that your roof was shipped yesterday. Yours truly, Montgomery Ward." What a short letter. Perhaps mine had been too long. But what a grand letter. I swore they would never regret their decision. What a wonderful and well managed organization they were to allow their managers to put aside rules and use their own judgement. Real gratitude filled my heart.

The staff was as thrilled as I, and soon the smell of hot tar replaced that old damp plaster. Long rolls of pretty green roofing were stuck together with tar like glue. Everyone in town could see that the hotel had a new hat. How nice it would look with a feather up the front — a bright neon sign. But that could wait. For the present, let it rain, let it snow or sleet. We were safe and dry inside.

Afterword

Florence Means made a success of the hotel. According to her daughter, Laura Means Pope, her success lay in running the hotel as if it were her home, with "total hospitality and great warmth." In the evening, for instance, she would often play the piano in the lobby and the guests would sing songs. Laura Pope also remembers that she and her sister Frances loved to play "dress-up" and would put on "fashion shows" for the guests. Many of the guests were "regulars," who would drive far out of their way to stay at the hotel. "They were equipment salesmen, government agents, etcetera," recalls Laura Pope. "These traveling businessmen loved the homey atmosphere and welcome."

To improve the dining room, Florence Means removed the booths and moved the counter to an inside wall next to the entrance. This meant that the waitresses trekked far-ther from the kitchen to serve the counter, but workmen could slip into a counter seat for fast service without the embarrassment of walking past better-dressed diners at the tables. Tablecloths and flowers, in season, graced those tables.

To enhance the view from the dining room window, Florence Means planted geraniums and other flowers. In training waitresses, she told them: "Now I want you to treat each customer as if your job depended on it — because it does." After three years of running the hotel, every room was filled almost every night. If there were too many guests, Florence directed the overflow to the homes of friends.

In 1936 Frank Means was appointed manager of the Colorado State Fair, and in 1938 the family moved to Pueblo. In that year Florence Means also sold the Saguache Hotel to Zoe Hazard, who had recently separated from Herbert Hazard.

According to family members, Florence made a profit of $10,000. She was paid $5,000 in cash and given title to three rental buildings on Saguache's main street: the Public Service building, the only liquor store, and the only garage. Uncomfortable owning the liquor store, she soon sold that building.

The cash profit and rental properties gave Florence Means a modicum of financial independence. Her subsequent adventuring included learning to fly a Piper Cub in 1944,[14] attending the University of Mexico the summer of 1946, and traveling to a still war-torn Europe in 1948. And, probably much to her relief, she was able to contribute substantially to the education expenses of Laura Belle and Frances without having to teach piano as she had done for Marjorie's edu-

---

[14] According to Laura Pope,"Mom never got a private pilot's license because she refused to put the plane into a spin without the instructor in it. At that time, to get a private pilot's license you had to take the plane up, spin it three times to the right, recover altitude, spin it three times to the left, and land it — all in sight of the state tester before he would get into the plane to give the rest of the test.

cation. As a result of their involvement with the state fair, the Meanses became friends with a variety of clowns, cowboys, carnival people, and entertainers. "It was a liberal education, and we learned a great respect for show people," Florence recalled.

When Frank Means retired as state fair manager in 1950, he and Florence moved to "Elmstead," a charming old adobe house on a small acreage outside of Pueblo. There Frank's small herd of purebred sheep produced lambs that 4-H youngsters would raise and show under his guidance. He also remained active in both the National Wool Marketing Corporation and the Colorado Wool Marketing Corporation. He served as president of the later group for 25 years. After Frank's death in 1968, Florence moved to an apartment in downtown Colorado Springs where she lived until her death in 1973.

The Saguache Hotel has changed little since the 1930s. One still enters the hotel by crossing a wooden boardwalk. The rooms where the hotel help once lived have now been turned into a long bar. The guest rooms upstairs haven't changed at all. Except for the one room with a private bath, guests must still trudge to the facilities at the end of the hall. Walls are paper thin. Each room has its original corner washbasin and radiator. Each door still has a working transom. The hotel has had a succession of owners, and as of spring, 1992, was closed and again for sale.

The little-changed hotel, as well as the Horace Means house, was used as a set in the TV movie, "Land of Little Rain," the story of the writer Mary Austin's life in the California desert town of Independence. The movie was filmed in the summer of 1987 and featured as a PBS American Playhouse Production. Renamed the "Independence Hotel" for the movie, the Saguache Hotel still displays the movie-set sign.

Saguache was ideal as a turn-of-the century movie set, for it has escaped the shock-inducing rapid change of so many places in America. In fact, it joins the long list of communities that appear to be fighting for survival in a speeded-up age. Many services and amenities were probably much better a half-century ago. Saguache, however, continues to hold onto one amenity any community might envy: a locally owned newspaper. Published since 1880, The Saguache Crescent *remains the only newspaper in Colorado still using a hot-metal process on a flatbed press, according to publisher Dean Coombs.*

The Means' home ranch is now the site of an organic farm that specializes in such high-altitude crops as quinoa, a grain widely used for centuries by Peruvians. The sheep pens are quiet.

In 1913 Florence and Frank Means spent their honeymoon on a horseback trip in the Colorado mountains. Throughout her life, Florence was both adventurous and fun-loving.

A profit from the sale of the Saguache Hotel gave Florence Means some of her own money. The hotel venture thus made possible new ventures, including learning to fly an airplane at age 51.

Someday, the hotel, that white elephant, would carry us to the very doors of the Metropolitan.

IN THE SWIRL
OF THE UNIVERSE

I went to the hotel each morning except Friday and Sunday. Friday was cleaning day, but more important, it was Walter Damrosch day. At ten o'clock we would turn off the sweeper, turn on the radio, and hear the great maestro say, "Good morning my dear children." No doubt the program was intended for school children, but thousands of other housewives and I were surely his dear children.[15]

No one conducted Wagner with as much understanding as did Damrosch. He was the first person to introduce me to the "Flight of the Valkyries." He explained that Valkyries were angels who came on white steeds to transport fallen warriors from the battlefield to heaven. We must listen for the neigh of the horses, he said, and give ourselves to the flight.

---

[15] Walter Johannes Damrosch (1862–1950), a well known conductor of both opera and symphony, was appointed musical adviser to NBC in 1927. He subsequently developed the Music Appreciation Hour for schoolchildren in the United States and Canada.

Then the orchestra set the pace of a galloping horse. It was exactly like one, not just the uneven beat of hoofs but the actual lift of the saddle and rhythmic swing of the body. The flight began. Powerful, lunging phrases carried one upward, always upward, climbing through the heavens. One could imagine distended nostrils, flying manes, and even hear the sharp neighing in the music. The very swirl of the universe was there. On and on they flew, joined from time to time by other mounting steeds. These were no phantom horses. They had weight and strength to carry them on. The music grew wilder, more powerful and exciting. Ida and I sat on the edge of the davenport and were fancifully whisked through the spheres.[16]

Finally a broad cadence drew rein on the cavalcade. Majestic chords announced the approach to heaven, the music of Heaven. Tears came to my eyes. Surely nothing but music could give even a hint of that celestial paradise. Pearly gates and streets of gold had never meant anything to me.

Another morning Mr. Damrosch played the slumber music from the same opera. Brunhilde, leader of the Valkyries, had disobeyed her father, Wotan, king of the gods. As punishment, he had cast a spell upon her, putting her to sleep on a mountain top and surrounding her with a ring of fire. Only the one courageous enough to brave this conflagration should awaken her, he declared. The fire music was woven with the slumber music in such a beautiful duet of darting flames and undulating sleepiness that one could easily imagine the lovely blonde goddess prone in her armor, completely surrounded by flames.

---

[16] Ida Burch helped Florence Means both at the hotel and at home. According to payroll records, she received $30 a month in wages plus board.

To think that such spectacles were actually portrayed at the Metropolitan Opera House in New York gave me a determined ambition. My children and I would someday sit and behold these wonders. True enough, we lived on a sheep ranch, we were having hard times, but we would study now and work hard. Then someday, the hotel, that white elephant, would carry us to the very doors of the Metropolitan. We'd wear long dresses, stay at a nice hotel, and sit in a maze of wonderment, absorbing through every sense, the vision that was Wagner's. I vowed it.

I composed a letter to Miss Bishop, the librarian at the University of Colorado. I told her of our hunger for a better understanding of opera, especially Wagner. She sent a book by Gertrude Hall which exactly answered our need. This book gave such an interesting and delightful story of the Ring operas that we were soon absorbed in legends, arias, and motifs. The children were quick to recognize the approach of Loge, the fire god, whose motif was like a tongue of flame darting up the chimney. They knew the sword motif and the lordly dignified approach of Wotan.

On Saturday afternoon, the children and I would sit around the fireplace completely absorbed in the radio opera. If anyone came to the door or called on the phone, they were apt to get a curt response. Our greatest disturber was the pump. Our water supply was dependent upon an electric pump, and the grinding of that motor completely drowned out the broadcasts. If the men happened to be watering the sheep, it would black out whole scenes. I shall never forget our frustration and exasperation when that grind started just as Wolfram in *Tannhauser* began "Oh, Thou Sweet Evening Star." We were so upset that we had to laugh to keep from crying.

After our Saturday operas we often enjoyed a cup of chocolate and cookies. We'd talk about our trip to New York and decided to buy seats for the whole Ring, four operas. We'd see it all, from the Rhinemaidens teasing the little dwarfs, to the scene where the great white horse jumped into the fire of Gotterdammerung. It seemed they had a white horse who really did leap into the fire. And the Rhine overflowed. The children wondered how they kept it from coming right out over the audience.

Sometimes Frank joined us for refreshments. He enjoyed music, but was more interested in the fact that Walter Damrosch's aunt and uncle had once lived in Saguache than he was in the Flight of the Valkyries.[17]

---

[17] In 1942 Florence Means took Frances and Laura Belle to Dallas to see the Metropolitan Opera perform *Carmen* and *Aida*. We do not know if she ever saw a performance of *The Ring*. In their later years Florence's Saturday afternoon opera was likely to conflict with Frank's television viewing of football games. But they reached an amicable compromise. Frank watched the television with no sound, and Florence listened to the opera.

PIANO RECITAL

COMMUNITY CHURCH

May 10, 1935, 8 O'clock P. M.

Duet, March .... Herbert Sanders
Ruth and John Greer Martin
The Big Bass Singer .... Walter Rolfe
Harold Gross
Wooden Shoe Dance .... James H. Rogers
Laura Belle Means
Valse Minature .... Montague Ewing
Ruth Martin
The March of the Boy Scouts .... N. Louise Wright
John Greer Martin
In Old Vienna .... Arranged by Margaret Anderson
Mary Emma Woodard

The Black Bird's Song .... Cyril Scott
Miss Frances Millikan

Sailor Boy .... T. Robin Mac Lachlan
Glenn Melvin Coleman
The Holland Festival .... Michael Aaron
Peggy Anderson
The Jovial Gypsy .... Theodora Dutton
Mary Emma Hagan
Jubilee March .... Fredrick Williams
Doris Dilley
Dance of the Leaves .... Marie Seuel Holst
Marjorie Johnson
Cinderella .... Robert Kuhn
Irene Davey
Community March .... Fredreck Williams
Helen Johnson
Spanish Dance .... Moretz Moskowske
Laura Crow
Narcissus .... Ethelbert Nevin
Elizabeth Sickler
The Fountain .... C. Bohm
Helen Rominger

Ah, Sweet Mystery of Life .... Victor Herbert
Helen Marie Ritzsinger

Duet, The Little Birds Longing .... Max Lenecke
Mary Emma Woodard and Helen Rominger
Berceuse .... Moretz Moszkowski
Barbara Slane
Bells of St. Mary's .... Edward St. Quentin
Irwin Means
Sextette from Lucia .... D. Durg
Marjorie Woodard
Polish Dance .... Xaver Scharwenka
Shirley Jean Curtis
Valcik .... John Mokrejs
George H. Hazard
The Flight of the Bumble Bee .... N. Rimsky Korsakov
Jane Hazard
En Route .... Pahmgren
Lois Ogden
Duet, Glow Worm .... Paul Lencke
Shirley Curtis and Marjorie Woodard

Although Florence Means loved music, she found teaching piano an exhausting experience. Needing the money, however, she taught from 1930 to 1935. Above is the program of her last student recital in May, 1935.

"Lady, lady, are you not the friend of the gypsies?"

THE COMING
OF THE GYPSIES

The first experience we had with gypsies at the ranch was with a band that came through in covered wagons, driving a few head of horses to trade. While we were at breakfast one morning, we saw two men coming up the hill with a very small wagon drawn by two very skinny horses. The men looked like brigands. One wore two long pistols in his belt, and the others glowered from behind long dark mustaches, but their outfit looked harmless — almost juvenile in fact. The little wagon was small and low, not much larger than a play wagon.

They wanted hay. Just a little jag.[18] So Frank accepted fifty cents and showed them where the stack yard was. Unfortunately for the gypsies they had to come back past the house when they were loaded. We looked out in utter amazement. It was impossible to believe that anyone could load that

---

[18] A dialect word meaning a small load.

much hay on a good-sized wagon to say nothing of that one. It looked like a whole hay stack rolling by. Frank dashed out of the house yelling for them to stop.

"What do you think you're doing? Hauling off the whole ranch? You told me you wanted a jag. What do you think hay is worth?"

Slowly the gypsies turned around, muttering to themselves, and Frank came back to his breakfast, still fuming.

"Aren't you afraid to talk like that to men with two guns?" I asked. "Certainly not," he said. "When a man gets so he's afraid to run his own business, he'd better quit."

A few years later, the gypsies who came through were driving Cadillacs and Packards. By then I had learned more about them.

A delightful book, *Lavengro* by George Borrow, had first awakened my interest in gypsies.[19] *Engro,* it seems, means 'maker of' in Romany and *Lav* means horseshoes. Then a current book, *Gypsy Fires of America* by Irving Brown, had further augmented my curiosity about these transient peoples.[20] They drove into town in their high-powered cars, disgorged dozens of children who had been lying on top of their feather beds and luggage, and in a twinkle a laundry of colored prints would be hanging on the fence. While the older women cooked supper, the men relaxed in groups and the younger women went swinging gracefully toward town in their full long skirts to beg, pilfer, or tell fortunes.

The women make the living in gypsydom, it seems — horse trading and violin playing being the only known

---

[19] First published in London in 1851, *Lavengro* was available in many editions, including Everyman Library.

[20] Brown, Irving. *Gypsy Fires of America,* 1930.

occupations of a gypsy male. He is detached, dark of expression and haughty. The women are loquacious, light-fingered, and busy. It makes a very workable combination, and they both share the love for travel on the open road. In this I concurred.

The phone rang one evening to tell me that the gypsies were in town.

"I surely hope they don't leave before I get down to see them," I replied.

"Well, I guess you're the only one in town who feels that way," was the answer.

From our front windows we could look down at the encampment. It was too late in the evening to call on them, but each time I looked out the window I could see a bonfire burning and figures moving about in front of its light. As soon as I could manage it, I would surely go to call.

The next morning, having first emptied my coat pockets, I started out. I carried a bucket of buttermilk to take to a friend. I hurried until I approached the gypsies then slowly walked by. Two young girls said, "Good morning." They were lovely looking — fairer than most of the race and both graceful and gay. One wore an amber necklace of great length and beauty, and I knew from my reading that their jewels were real.

I stopped, and they came to the fence to talk.

"Oh, lady, what have you in your pail? Milk?"

I nodded.

"Oh lady, you give milk to the poor gypsies. I have a tiny new baby."

"Just came last week," added her friend.

They begged with such charm and appeal that we all three enjoyed it.

"I think you have no baby," I said, "because you are not married. You do not wear the *diklo*."

Instantly they glanced at each other.

"You speak Romany?" they asked in excitement. "Very little," I replied honestly. "But I know that a married gypsy wears a *diklo*." This is the head scarf. "And I know too, that you are not poor. You need not beg my milk because you are richer than I. Look at those beads."

They smiled with pleasure and called more women to come to meet the *gadjo*.

"I understand *gadjo*," I said. "That means enemy does it not?"

"No, no — not enemy. It means a — a stranger. Yes, stranger," with gentle reassurance.

They were trying to be kind to me, for certainly I had thought gypsies spoke of a *gadjo* in the same tone that a regular army man speaks of a civilian. Certainly a thing apart.

We stood and visited while the group enlarged. More women and children gathered around, and one of the girls lifted her blouse to show me the pocketbook fastened to her belt. Small coins were sewed to it, and when I admired them she let me hold a small gold coin marked 1735.

Then one of the older women invited me in to see their pressure cookers and beds. I was allowed to feel the pillows and beds of down, and I surely did admire their big aluminum cookers.

The men sitting around the stove scarcely glanced at me. The only time they paid me the slightest attention was when I asked where they were from.

One older man spoke up. "We are from Buenos Aires."

"Indeed!" I said. "You came by boat to New Orleans?"

"No, we came to New York and are driving to California."

"Did you stop in Chicago? On Halsted street?"

One woman answered quickly: "Yes, yes. You know Halsted Street?"

"No, I do not. But I know that many gypsies live there and that the Canadian gypsies winter there. I have always wanted to go to see them."

Finally when I said I must go, an older woman came up and said, "Now let me tell your fortune!"

"But I have no money — I emptied my pockets for fear you would get it." And we all laughed. "Then let me tell your fortune for nothing," she said.

I stood surrounded by gypsy women and children while she held my hand in hers. She did not look into my hand but into my face as she said seriously: "You are a good woman. You love all people. You are not afraid. You will have much happiness all your life." And we parted.

The next day I was driving down to the hotel when a gypsy man ran out to stop me. In great excitement he called, "Lady, lady, are you not the friend of the gypsies?"

"Yes, I am," as I slowed to a stop.

"Tell me, do you know the sheriff?"

"Yes, I do."

"Is he your friend?"

"I hope so."

"They have one of our women in jail."

"What for?"

"Nothing, lady, Nothing. Will you please see the sheriff and tell him to let her out of the jail?"

"But what did she do?"

"She do nothing. Please! Will you talk to him, lady? Tell him it is very bad to have the gypsies in town so long, begging at all the houses."

I smiled and added, "And stealing all the chickens!"

Quick as a wink he joined in, "Yes, and stealing all the chickens."

"I am going to the hotel now and will speak to him."

When Slim sauntered down the stairs soon afterward, I asked, "Slim! What are you doing to my gypsies?"

"Oh, it's not my fault," he said. "I had a call from Salida to arrest the whole bunch and bring them back for trial."

"But what did they do?"

"Oh, you know that old game. 'You put your hands on me and I'll put mine on you while I tell your fortune?' Well some old geezer fell for it, and she got his wallet with seventy-five dollars in it."

"Well it's a shame to arrest them. Anyone should know enough to be on their guard with gypsies."

Slim grinned and said, "At least you'd have thought that after he got taken in, the old fool would have kept still about it."

But the long arm of the law got justice. The gypsies were fined heavily and had to sell their jewels to pay the fine. They had their own channels of exchange and were finally freed. But I always thought Salida must have a crooked stick of some kind placed along the highway which meant in Romany: "Beware of this place. People in Saguache are more friendly."

*These gypsy women at a funeral in Denver in 1915 were
similar to those Florence Means encountered in Saguache.
Unlike many, she felt both curiosity and good will toward
the itinerants. (Western History Department, Denver
Public Library)*

One of the greatest thrills of my whole lifetime came after I had set thirteen eggs under a nice big hen.

THE THRILL
OF CHICKENS
(An Oral Reminiscence)

When I first came to Saguache, I would go to parties and play bridge, and all my friends would talk about their chickens and how many chickens had hatched. And I had no chickens. My husband was prejudiced against them for some reason. He had been told that chickens carry diseases to sheep and to cattle. But I kept asking for chickens, and he kept refusing. And I would have to listen to my friends talking about their chickens.

Then fortune favored me. A hired man came to our ranch and brought his own chickens. And Frank permitted them because he had to have the man and couldn't tell him not to bring them. So I said, "Well, if a hired man can have chickens, certainly I can have chickens." So at long last Frank built a chicken house. He dug it into the ground about two feet so the wind would not blow in on the floor. It was warm and nice and up against the granary.

Well, Frank was still suspicious. "You know nothing about chickens," he said. "How will you know to take care of them?"

"Well," I said, "I will send to Washington D.C. and get the folders and books that tell about it."

And that's just what I did. You have no idea the number of diseases chickens can have. I just read pages and pages about all the things that can happen to chickens. I could see that perhaps Frank had had a point.

But I got along very well with the chickens. We had a nice big yard, fenced-in. I used to take an apple box and just go out and watch the chickens. They're so happy; they would sing and call. And I'd sit on the apple box and watch them. They were beautiful. I named them all. I had Geraldine, I had Leona — I had them all named after my friends. But then one day Wilson Williams came to visit me. He was a chicken fan. He said, "Now listen, Florence. There's one thing I'm going to tell you now. You must stop naming your chickens because to be a successful chicken raiser you must replace them every two years. After that they eat more feed then they produce, and they don't make any money. You have to sell them or eat them and replace them with young chickens." So I had to give up naming my chickens.

One of the greatest thrills of my whole lifetime came after I had set thirteen eggs under a nice big hen, after making a nice nest for her. She was very faithful and wouldn't object when I would go down near her, like setting hens do. When I went out the morning the eggs were supposed to hatch, which I recall takes just three weeks, I put my hand under the hen. And there, every egg had hatched! There were thirteen baby chickens under her. That was one of the greatest thrills of my lifetime. You people who buy your chickens from an incubator and then raise them, they're nice I'm sure, and you're proud of them, but you have no idea what a thrill it is to raise chickens as I did.

And so through the years I got the first prize on my rooster at the county fair. And I did have so many lovely eggs all the time for the family.

But my little boy and husband were the kind that couldn't let me just go boasting to everybody about my chickens. One morning I went out — and, oh my, there were so many eggs. I was so excited and put them in a bucket. Then in a couple of hours I went out again, and there were more eggs. So I brought in all those eggs. And I said, "Oh, Frank, look how many eggs I'm getting today. Look how my chickens are laying. My friends aren't getting any eggs at all to speak of." After a couple hours I'd run out again and find more eggs. Finally I was so excited I began to call my friends, and I even called the hotel and asked if they could use extra eggs. They said they'd be very happy to have any I didn't use.

That evening as I was talking to the family, I said, "You know, I think I have more eggs than chickens." Then Frank said, "Oh, no, you just have more chickens than you realize. Have you counted them lately?" "Well, no," I said, "but they are doing well." Then he and my little boy put their arms around me. "Do you know what day this is?" they asked. And I said, "No, why?" And they said, "This is April First."

Those two rascals had been running out to the chicken house putting eggs in the nest, and then when I'd bring them in they'd replace the eggs in the bucket with paper, leaving a few eggs on top. And then they'd run out, putting more eggs in the nest, and watch me bringing them in with such glee and excitement. So that evening I had but a bucket full of paper, and I had to call the hotel and say I had made a mistake, that I didn't have as many eggs as I thought I had.

And I didn't know eagles would eat chickens!

PREY AND PRANK
(An Oral Reminiscence)

We had a lovely dinner club in Saguache, which we took turns hosting. We had a habit that when one woman was the hostess, one of the others would bring the prize for the person with the best bridge score. And it was also always something big. One time it would be a lovely cake or a batch of cookies. It was always a treat and joy to win the prize.

But one winter the boys decided they would bring the prize. I remember the time that the prize Wilson Williams brought was a batch of cold pancakes. So they were being mischievous and naughty.

One day when Frank was driving home, he saw an eagle, and the eagle had just eaten a jack rabbit. After an eagle has eaten all it can possibly hold, it can hardly get off the ground. Frank could see it was having difficulty getting into the air, so he quickly jumped out of the pickup and got his sheep hook and caught the eagle. Well, it was a great big beautiful bird. Frank brought him home and put him in the granary, next to the chicken house. But the granary had a little hole in the bottom door, where I allowed my little chickens to go in and out. And I didn't know eagles would eat chickens! I don't know how many chickens I lost because the chickens would go in to get grain, and the eagle would eat them. I didn't realize what was happening.

Well, Frank kept the eagle there for a couple of weeks, I guess. The boys decided to give that as the prize when we next had dinner club at the Woodwards. When the day came, Frank put the eagle in a big crate and left him on the porch at the Woodwards. Then the boys decided that Daisy [Ashley] should win the prize. So when they played against her, they would overbid purposely. They would overbid and go set, and Daisy would just keep getting a bigger score and bigger score. And there was no possible chance that anyone could win but Daisy. So finally when she won the prize, they went out onto the porch and brought in this crate with a great big eagle in it. OH, she was so upset and so distressed. And Ray Woodward said, "Well, Frank, that's a great note for you to bring a prize like that. When everybody else brings a prize, they bring a lovely cake or pies, and you bring an old buzzard." After everyone had enjoyed the joke, they took the eagle outdoors and let him free.

*A common sight on the Means ranch in summertime was
stacking hay — as long as the thunderstorms stayed away.*

"Well, I'll be damned. A woodpecker must have done that."

WOODWARD'S WOODPECKER

(An Oral Reminiscence)

One time Mary Woodward was in Denver, and Ray was at home asleep on a Sunday morning. He was awakened by a dreadful noise — Ra-ta-tat-ta, Ra-ta-tat-ta. It sounded like a woodpecker making a hole in the house. So Ray opened the window and shooed the bird away.

Then he got back in bed when Ra-ta-tat-ta, Ra-ta-tat-ta — there was that old bird again. By now Ray was so upset, he got out of bed in his pajamas, took his gun and went outside and shot the bird. Well, they had a shingle bungalow, and when he got back in the house, to his dismay, there were feathers, plaster, and all sorts of debris strewn over the bed. He had shot right through the wall of his house.

Well, that really upset him, so he took a picture that was hanging on the wall and hung it over the hole. Then he brushed off the bed as best he could and went back to sleep. Some days later Mary was combing her hair at the dressing table when, in the mirror, it looked as if the picture back of her was moving. She turned around to see if it was, and it seemed to be quiet, and so she started to brush her hair again. Again in the mirror she was sure she saw the picture move. So she went over to the wall and picked up the picture. There she discovered the wind was blowing through a big hole and making the picture move back and forth. About that time Ray came in, and she said, "Come here, Ray. Come in here in the bedroom. And she took him over to show him the hole. "Well, I'll be damned," he said. "A woodpecker must have done that."

A Selected Correspondence 1935–1936

Readers of Florence Means' stories have been disappointed not to find the same style and flair in her letters. It's true. The letters are nowhere as entertaining as the stories, but they are included because they provide a grounding of fact and detail for those interested in the hotel itself and in the reality of life for the Means family in 1935 and 1936. From the letters we get a sense of the pervading worries about money. We also get a picture of a "modern woman," a woman seeking to balance the demands of family, home, and community life with those of earning money and nourishing her own spirit. It is a search well known to each of Florence's three daughters as well as to their daughters.

Florence Means wrote often during the school year to her daughter Marjorie ("Marmie") at the University of Colorado in Boulder. Marjorie, who graduated in June 1936, ran the hotel when her mother made a trip to the Northwest in the fall of 1936. No correspondence exists between them for 1937 and 1938, for by then Marjorie was married to John Cogswell and living in Saguache.

FIRST MENTION OF THE HOTEL: It's interesting how close in spirit and detail this 1935 letter is to the 1972 reminiscence.

April 15 [1935]

Dearest Marnie,

. . . Now I have something else to tell you. It became necessary for Daddy to take back the hotel . . . Herbert Hazard debated about buying it but found it in terrible condition. Then Daddy just about decided to nail it up — which is bad for the town.

I said, "If I'll manage it will you let me have it?" and he said "Yes!" I said "If I can sell it can I have the money?" and he said "Absolutely!" Now dear it seems like a big undertaking and very foreign to my nature but if I sit still . . . and let it be sold for taxes when I might make ten thousand dollars am I not a quitter? It will be a good excuse to get rid of my music class. I'm so weary teaching, as I always am in the spring.

I'll keep the house open and you can manage that. If you want to teach you can no doubt have all the pupils you want. I'll keep a girl here and you can keep an eye on the children. I'll try to arrange to be here evenings and part of the afternoon. Mr. and Mrs. Cummings, the "Fixit Man," will help me manage it. He'll repair and paint the whole place so I can sell it at a good price. I've already arranged with them. She'll do the chamber-work and laundry. I have no cook yet but will get one. I don't want you and the children at the hotel. I may move down there this winter but not while the children can play outside. They need a home.

Daddy is very busy with his cattle & sheep and cannot be bothered with a hotel. I believe I can sell it to Herbert Hazard in a few years and we'll all go to Europe. You can see how I dream. I may make a failure of it but isn't it better to fail after a try at it than just let it go by default? . . .

Daddy didn't ask me to do this. He said he never would. But if it's mine no telling how it may turn out.

Write me what you think.

PATERNAL ADVICE: It was clearly a struggle for Florence to be caught between her father's opinion and what she wanted to do.

Friday eve
[Posted April 27, 1935]

Dearest Marmie —
 ... I'm afraid the hotel business is off. My father thinks its out of the question. He just the same as said that I had two small children and had better stay home and take care of them. I feel upset. I hate to do it against his advice and still I'd love to take hold there. I just have a feeling that it will work out for the best some way. Perhaps Daddy will sell it after all. But it looks as though I'll be home this summer ...

MAKING ARRANGEMENTS: We don't know why Florence decided to ignore her father's advice, but within the next two weeks she had taken over the hotel.

Friday evening
We're having a wonderful snow today —
[Posted May 4, 1935]

Dearest Marmie —
 ... I think I'm having the hotel after all with Donald as manager. He'll go in on June first. I think he'll be fine for it ...

Saturday May 11, 1935

Dearest Marmie
 ... I'm taking the hotel. Herbert is loaning me enough money to pay back taxes etc. Donald will be here next week to look things over. We go in the first of June.

HOME AND HOTEL: This was a long letter for Florence, one that captures some of the complexity and enthusiasms of her life.

[Posted May 26, 1935]

Dearest Marmie —

Sunday evening with the radio on, Daddy reading his "Time," Kim at his feet. Laura Belle reading, Frances, a little indisposed from overeating, and a hundred baby chicks under the stove. That's the picture. I was supposed to get fifty chickens three weeks old for which I was to pay ten dollars. When I got there I couldn't get any. They have no excuse — just said they didn't have them. I was a little disappointed as I have only nine hens and had been planning to eat them. Then the man said, "If you'll take a hundred baby chicks you can have them for eight dollars." So I couldn't resist the bargain . . .

We've had very damp cold weather. More rain than any May I can remember. A strange thing has happened. The sea gulls have come. The ranch is dotted with their white bodies and they soar over the house. You'd think we were fifty miles from the ocean. There was an article in the paper about their being seen near Alamosa and we have fifty or a hundred on the ranch all the time. The Mexican herders saw them but didn't know what they were. It's a strange thing isn't it? Do you suppose they just followed the heavy rain clouds from the ocean? They seem to dig worms and follow the irrigation ditches. They look very much out of place here. I wish you could ask some professor about it.

. . . I haven't started to clean house yet. It's too disagreeable and we have a fire in the furnace all the time. I'll be able to get it done before you get home I hope. I've been so interested in the hotel that I haven't thought about house cleaning at home.

Esther Anderson is cooking at the hotel. The Conn girls waitresses. Mr. Cummings Janitor, Mrs. Cummings, housekeeper. Donald desk man — not a bad line up is it? I hope we can make a go of it. We'll surely try. Donald is full of enthusiasm.

You'll have to help me manage at home although I won't really be down at the hotel. Donald is boss . . .

MONEY WORRIES: In all the detail about money coming in and going out, this letter captures Florence's need to count every penny and her frustration in not having enough money to do what she considered important. It's also interesting to learn that she was in debt to the hotel, a bill Donald asked her to pay.

Friday evening
[Posted October 26, 1935]

Dearest Marmie —

So many times when I have planned to visit you something has happened to prevent it at the last minute and it almost happened today. One time the car broke and several times, at the last minute Daddy would say I couldn't afford it. Remembering this, I saved out the most of last month's music money. I took in nearly fifty dollars and out of it paid Laura Belle's violin lessons, five dollars to Knight Campbell —the children's roller skates etc. and had thirty-eight dollars left. The tickets to the concert were $6.60 for two and I gladly sent it off leaving a little over thirty.

I had paid something on your dress, and coat, and fifteen dollars to Fishers out of my allowance but I had been unable to pay the hotel — I [admit] I'd let it run a bit. Well our new roof is coming and the freight is $50 so Donald asked me if I could pay my bill. It had run for two months and was $33 — just a bit more than I had. So I told him how it all was and he was sweet about it. I paid him $20 which leaves me about eleven dollars for the trip. I feel a bit shaky about it but am coming anyway. I thought in a pinch you might pay me five or ten dollars on your clothes now that you are a bit ahead. I paid about twenty-five dollars on your clothes this month. Perhaps I can get by on the eleven. But I've counted so on seeing you that I'm coming.

Perhaps tomorrow I can joke about it but tonight it seemed quite tragic. You can't answer this as I'll be there so soon.

DOING TOO MUCH: Like many of us, Florence found that even a short trip from home can help identify priorities. Learning to say no, however, did not come easily to either Florence or Marjorie. A generation later Marjorie was saying the same thing to her daughters.

Sunday eve
[Posted November 4, 1935]

Dearest Marmie —

I got home safely about ten o'clock Friday night. I drove rather slowly and had no flat tires. After leaving you I stopped at the garage for the tire I had had repaired . . . I felt that my trip was rather rushed in many ways and still I accomplished the major thing I had in mind.

. . . I taught nine music lessons yesterday which will help pay all the bills I incurred. I didn't get my suitcase unpacked until late last night.

Today Sunday I dressed three chickens — sold two to Margaret Curtis for $1.90, took the milk to the hotel — washed the children's hair, made a batch of doughnuts, did my little washing and as Daddy has gone down town I decided to write you.

It was so good to see you and I worry because you do so much. But I believe we'll just have to side step things. Donald wanted me to come to the hotel and I decided not to. Then both Miss Ritzsinger and the preacher phoned me to come to church to hear some special music, but I didn't go. I think we'll just have to learn to say no to unimportant things.

MANAGING THE HOTEL: It's clear that at first Florence had really depended on Donald to manage the hotel. But as the next two letters indicate, Donald fell below expectations. It's at this point that Florence takes over the active management of the hotel.

Sunday
[Posted December 9, 1935]

Dearest Marmie,

Yesterday I wrote you a very bad explosive letter but today I feel better so will not send it. I was away from home every night last week. Monday — teachers, Tuesday Dinner Club, Wednesday teaching, Thursday Choral Club, Friday Teachers. The babies were so homesick for me that last night after I'd taught eleven lessons they wanted to celebrate Mother's being home. I bought some marshmallows and assorted nuts and brought up apples — we turned on the radio, had a fire in the fireplace and they were as excited as could be. It was a real party. Well, we just got going good when the phone rang and Jack and Mrs. Scholler were in town and said they'd be right up. You should have seen the babies — They were so disappointed. Well today I tried to make it up to them. We went riding with Daddy to buy some new bulls, then we went to see Shirley Temple in Curly Locks and then to the hotel to dinner.

. . . I'm taking over the active management of the hotel Jan 1st or as soon as you leave. Donald isn't very well and may go to Arizona. Or he may stay at the hotel . . .

Monday
[Posted January 8, 1936]

Dearest Marmie,

. . . I worked in the hotel this morning. H—— is leaving, for which I am thankful. The lobby hasn't been scrubbed for ten days and is filthy. I haven't decided just how I'll manage yet but will put Verna in front, I think. Donald is drunk about half the time so I'm glad he's going, too. I'm getting so I just hate drink. It's no wonder they lose their jobs.

Didn't we have a nice time in Denver? I told Daddy how we took a little spree and he seemed to understand. He wants us to,

I think. He's sweet as pie since I'm back and don't talk to you so much. He doesn't like competition when it comes to my interest. He's gone to Kiwanis Club tonight.

I'm so thankful for Ida. I could never run the hotel if I didn't have her. I'm going to pay her more since I'm gone so much . . .

THE BIG WORRY: Household and hotel money worries, of course, were nothing compared to the debt load Frank Means was carrying. Although in this letter and others, Florence mentioned moving to the hotel, she never did.

January 12, 1936

Dearest Marmie,

It is Sunday afternoon and Laura Belle and Frances are both lying down in the living room with slight temperatures. Frances went to school Monday and has been home in bed since. I called the doctor Thursday night and he seemed to do nothing. I'm watching her diet, giving her aspirin and cod liver oil. The only thing that worries me a good deal is that her ear aches. I surely hope it clears up.

Poor Daddy had quite a blow. The Wichita people turned his loan down. I don't know just how it will come out. The local Monte Vista P.C.A. [Production Credit Association] is going to try to make them reconsider. I do hope they don't force him to sell out now just as he might make some money. He can sell for enough to pay all his debts all right but he'd have very few sheep left to make a living with. I didn't sleep very well the first night I heard it, but I've decided that come what may I can take it. I think I'll move to the hotel as soon as Daddy comes from the stock show. That will save money both here and there. Donald left for Denver today . . .

When Donald balanced up the books he found that the hotel is a little better than breaking even, even though we're paying for all the improvements. I feel I'm going to make it dear — and sell one of these days . . .

104

NEW CONFIDENCE: Florence had undoubtedly been awed by the bookwork, but as she takes over the hotel she finds it's "no trick at all."

Thursday
[Posted January 24, 1936]

Dearest Marjorie:
. . . I go to the hotel each morning to keep books and it's no trick at all. Really I don't see why Donald thought it was such a job down there. It's nothing. As soon as Daddy comes home we're going to the hotel for a while. I think Donald has been sick so long that any trifle seems like a big job to him . . .

SWAMPED FOR TIME: We can't help but be impressed by everything Florence was doing — running the hotel, teaching piano lessons, writing her monthly article, managing a household with young children, raising and dressing chickens, etcetera. In this letter, however, we learn that Florence is giving up the piano teaching. That was made possible by two events: improving prospects at the hotel and reduced need as a result of Marjorie's imminent graduation from college.

March 3, [1936]

Dearest Marmie:
. . . I have been just swamped lately and haven't had time for letters. Last week I was out every night but one for one thing and another and of course the first of the month is a jam at the hotel. My books aren't balanced as yet. Then I taught eleven lessons Saturday, just finished one a minute ago and last night I stayed up until midnight to write my poem and article for the magazine [Colorado Wool Growers and Marketeer].
I'm giving up my class in May and am I glad. I've promised the children that if they'll be patient I'll take them to Taos the

day after the recital. I'm saving the Slonecker music money for the event. They need their mending done and their hair washed and I just can't find time to do everything. I got out all the hotel bills & music bills Sunday while Daddy and the children went to the show.

. . . The days are warm and sunny here. We've had no winter as yet and I'm glad. Summer will soon be here now. The house finches are building nests in the bushes and blue birds are here.

THE SMELL OF PROFIT: Florence was beginning to make money. It's also interesting to note that Frank Means (Daddy) was balancing the books. Now full of confidence, Florence hints that more than one person had doubted her ability to turn the hotel around. It was also characteristic of Florence to find an excuse for a "spree." The spree for her hotel staff was obviously a recognition for a job well done.

Saguache Colo
Sunday April 5 [1936]

Dearest Marmie

. . . Daddy just balanced the books for the month and I had made two hundred fifty dollars profit. I took in twelve hundred and sixty dollars in the month. I can't help but think of some of the remarks people have made . . . People were nasty. Even Donald gave up. Personally if it's going to pay two hundred dollars a month I don't care if it sells or not . . . I took my hotel staff on a spree. I took Esther, Aubrey, Eleanor, and Priscilla to Alamosa and Monte and then to the Walsh Hotel to dinner and to the show. It was a real treat for them and gave them some pointers as to how other hotels serve. It was such a cute show "Thirteen Hours in the Air." You must go to it. Zaza Pitts was one of the leading characters . . .

DISAPPEARING DEBTS: Frank Means may have not wanted to have anything to do with the hotel, but a year later, between balancing the books and giving advice, he was involved.

April 21, 1936

Dearest Marmie:
. . . The hotel is coming fine. The trouble is Donald wants to come back and Daddy is afraid he'll ruin things. I'm nearly out of debt and should be by the first of the month. I've just paid and paid on debts. This morning I finished paying Walton Ridgeway [owner of Saguache's department store]. I feel like I was working out a sentence . . .

QUESTIONABLE HELP: Nettie and Elmer Thayer were Florence's paternal aunt and uncle. As the next two letters indicate, she had great hopes in helping them at the same time as getting help for the hotel. As the second letter hints, these hopes were doomed to failure. Aunt Nettie and Uncle Elmer returned to the Northwest in the fall of 1936.

April 30, 1936

Dearest Marmie:
Aunt Nettie and Uncle Elmer are moving to Saguache to run the hotel. Isn't that grand? I heard through Lester [Florence's brother] that they were losing their ranch, so I phoned to Wenatchee at once. Then I wrote and told them how much I needed them and asked them to consider coming here. After a few weeks I had a letter saying they were heading for Saguache soon. I wrote them that I wanted to go to Commencement and hoped they'd get here to take over the management as soon as possible. Daddy [Florence's father, John Gellatly] wrote me that I would never know how much they appreciated my letter & call. They are so dear and have no children to turn to. So we'll all be

*their children. Aunt Nettie said she'd be here in time to help
with the trousseau, and she sews beautifully you know. I think it
will be ideal.*

*. . . I went to club today — must play for Choral Society
tonight and then work until midnight making out the bills . . .*

Tuesday

Dearest Marmie —

*. . . Aunt Nettie & Uncle Elmer arrived a week ago yesterday
and of course I had expected to turn the hotel over to them June
1st. But Uncle Elmer has been in bed ever since he arrived and I
am wondering if he'll ever be able to take it over. He is seventy-
two and just about at the end of his rope. He and Aunt Nettie
have no children so I am only glad to help them if I can. They
can live at the hotel and be near us.*

*The trouble is that I haven't cleaned house and probably can't
before I come to Boulder. But you and I can do it. We can do just
as we please, in fact. Won't it be fun to sew and read and
work? . . .*

MARJORIE TAKES OVER: By September, 1936, Marjorie has
finished college and takes over the hotel when Florence goes to visit
the Northwest. It is clear from the next two letters that, unlike her
mother, Marjorie had a penchant for meticulous bookkeeping. The
coming of the Russians, as mentioned at the end of the second
letter, was a big event in the family. Soviet representatives F. Volik
and Andrew J. Prudnikov bought all of Frank Means' prizewinning
rams in order to improve Russian sheep stock.

September 22 [1936]

[Dear Mother,]
Monday Sept 21 was a $32.00 day.

I deposited $28.00 and took $2.00 to pay Mr. Buckly for Daddy's pants.

We had Welsh Rarebit and sold 10 lunches. Novel lunches always sell better than others.

I had enough money to pay all the meat bills and Jones. It amounted to $42.00.

The linemen are here and Aubrey [Simpson] put them in 19. We had almost a full house last night and lots of the men are coming back tonight. Two men want to stay here for two weeks. Said they would let us know soon.

Today is a good day too.

That is all today.

Love,

Marjorie

P.S. The iron fireman or stocol [stokehole] or whatever it is arrived this morning and is very fine looking. Also Montgomery Ward was right about what you owed them. You hadn't entered it in the book.

October 2 [1936]

Dear Mother,
. . . The other night we had a full house, even the room with the telephone. Yesterday was a 32.00 day. The day before was a 39.00 day. I sent out bills for about 400.00. It isn't as much as I had hoped for but of course the teachers weren't here all the month. I don't have any too much money though. 167.00 to Roy Coleman is going to shrink the bank account. And I found out why I was overdrawn. You hadn't entered the check for Eleanor McKenzie at the first of the month. All the others were entered but not hers.

That made us 21.65 overdrawn that we didn't know about.

Today I cleaned out the invoices and found lots of little bills that I hope I can pay. Also I cleaned out the register and found 16.00 worth of checks dating from March. Some of them were people who had meal tickets, but had overcharged them. So I am sending those out tomorrow. 16.00 will pay a lot of little bills.

The stocol is in and works just grand. Aubrey says it uses lots less coal.

Well so much for the hotel.

. . . After I wrote the last letter to you, the Russians came back and spent the day with us. They ate lunch at the hotel and payed with a hundred dollar bill. Aubrey nearly fainted. And they talked to new York for nearly 10 minutes. . .

THE BOTTOM LINE: Although the hotel was beginning to make money, it is clear from this letter that Florence was still walking the line of indebtedness. She couldn't resist buying new things to improve the hotel.

October 6 [1936]
[Posted Wenatchee, Wash.]

Dearest Marjorie:

*Your letter just came and I am not as discouraged about the hotel as perhaps I should be. Most of my life in Saguache has been surmounting difficulties, anyway. I was sorry my bill at Fishers was so large. That's what one gets for letting everything get so run down. To have just **one** slip, two rather worn out pair of panties etc. demands a pay day someday, doesn't it?*

Daddy said he would pay you the $42 which you gave me to come on my trip so that will help. I really do not get enough allowance to manage decently for so many of us but we'll come out yet won't we dear?

I don't know how much money I'll need to come home on so think I'll not have you pay many bills. You might just pay Ida

*and the public service about fifteen dollars. I'll go to bat with
them over the sweeper. I think I'll write a $25.00 check
tomorrow. I know my parents are hard up and so I buy gasoline,
ice cream, shows and what I can to help.*

*. . . . I think the thing to do for the winter now is retrench —
do no more improving-no more painting — no more buying — I
knew September would show up badly for I bought about a
hundred dollars worth of things like rugs, sheets, cretonne
curtains, shades, spreads, etc. But with so many regulars it had to
be done. The place didn't really lose money dear. With you near
to talk things over with I'll forge ahead. A full house is all I can
ask and it seems to be full.*

*. . . I want to buy some Silex coffee pots for the hotel when I
get to Denver. No one uses those big urns anymore. No wonder
we have nicks [?]. It will cost about $20 to buy them so I won't
do it until I confer with you.*

INSIDE DETAILS: In the next two letters Marjorie gives some
interesting details about running the hotel. These are the last
letters of family correspondence until Florence and Frank move to
Pueblo in 1938. By then the hotel had been sold and the Saguache
chapter of their lives ended.

[Posted October 7, 1936]

Dear Mother,

*It's been several days since I've written you, but we've been so
busy. Tomorrow the American legion is going to have a dinner
for twenty. They decided to have the seventy-five cent chicken
dinner. We've planned a nice dinner with home made ice cream.
Some officers from Denver are coming. We're going to decorate
their table and plan things as nice as possible.*

*. . . We moved the bed from 24 up to 26 and put the
innerspring on it. We are having the dresser in 24 painted to
match it, so 26 will be attractive. In 24 we put the funny old*

111

green bed that was out in the shed and put that old innerspring on it. It sags on the sides. If anybody slept on the edge they'd fall out, but it is soft and comfortable for one person. If it is too bad, we will bring the springs down from the house.

Then we're going to fix up the store room. It will be a surprise.

My finances are coming along slowly but surely. I've paid $114 to help, made up an 82.00 overdraft, paid $32 light bill, a $30 meat bill and have $160 in the bank . . .

Florence Means stands with daughter Marjorie after her wedding in December 1936. The correspondence between Florence and Marjorie illuminates Florence's struggles and successes in running the hotel and in dealing with hard times.

 Some Saguache Recipes of Florence Means

The earliest recipes of Florence G. Means are written in an old, hardbound book with blank pages entitled *Recipes: My Friends and My Own.* Indeed, almost every recipe in this and her other recipe books credited the source, and almost always the source was a friend. Of the 71 recipes handwritten in this book, 37 focused on sweets — primarily cakes but also nut breads, ice cream, cookies, puddings, fudge, doughnuts, and marshmallows. Pickles or preserves account for 19 of the recipes. The remaining recipes included 5 salad recipes, 3 bread or roll recipes, 3 for meat dishes, and one each for lemonade, an omelet, popcorn balls, and "rose beads." These recipes, too, reflect an era that relied on home cooking, even at the hotel. Some of them continue to be family favorites.

NOTE: Few of these recipes come with mixing or baking directions. The experienced cook will know what to do; the inexperienced should be wary.

SQUASH OR PUMPKIN PIE

Mrs. Tillie Farrington

1 pint [winter] squash
1 pint milk [scalded]
3 eggs beaten
1 teaspoon vanilla
1 teaspoon nutmeg
1 teaspoon cinnamon
2 cups sugar

POTATO CAKE

Mrs. Gertrude Slane

2 cups sugar
1 cup butter
4 eggs
1/2 cup sweet milk
2 squares of chocolate melted over tea kettle
1 cup nuts
2 cups flour
2 teaspoons of baking powder
1 teaspoon each of cinnamon, cloves, nutmeg
1 cup mashed potatoes
1 teaspoon vanilla

MOCK ANGEL CAKE

Esther Anderson

1 1/2 cup cake flour
1 cup sugar
1 cup boiling milk
1 1/2 teaspoon baking powder
1/2 teaspoon salt
1 teaspoon vanilla
4 egg whites

Sift the flour & sugar together five times. Add the boiling milk & beat. Add the baking powder, vanilla, & salt. Fold in stiffly beaten egg whites. Bake in moderate oven.

DOUGHNUTS

Mrs. Bigg

1 egg
1 cup sugar
1 pinch salt
1 cup milk
Cinnamon & nutmeg
2 teaspoons baking powder
Flour

CARROT PUDDING

Marie Hazard

1 cup ground potatoes
1 cup carrots
1 cup sugar
1 cup ground suet
1 cup flour
1 cup ground raisins
1 cup nuts
1 teaspoon cinnamon
1/2 teaspoon allspice
1/2 teaspoon cloves
1/2 teaspoon salt
1 teaspoon soda dissolved in 2 tablespoons
  water
(A little baking powder may be added.)
Steam 2 hours.

LEMON ICE

Juice of six lemons, juice of one orange, three and a
half cups of sugar, five cups of water, whites of two
eggs whipped to a froth. Beat together and freeze
the same as ice cream.

SPICE CAKE

Mrs. Cochrane

1 cup sour milk
1 1/2 cups brown sugar
1 scant cup butter
2 eggs
2 cups flour
1 cup raisins floured
1 teaspoon nutmeg, cloves, cinnamon and soda
Bake slowly.

OATMEAL COOKIES

Mrs. Ridgeway

1 cup lard and butter
1 cup sugar
2 eggs
4 tablespoons of milk
2 cups flour
1 teaspoon cinnamon
3/4 teaspoon soda
1/2 teaspoon salt
2 cups rolled oats
1 cup raisins
1/2 cup nuts
Drop a little in spots on pans without grease.

SOFT GINGERBREAD

1 cup brown sugar
1 cup molasses
1/2 cup melted lard
3 eggs
2 cups flour
1 teaspoon salt and spices to taste
2/3 cup boiling water with 1 teaspoon soda
    dissolved in it, added last and well beaten in.

WATERMELON PICKLES

Mrs. I. Gotthelf

1 tablespoon salt to 1 quart of water poured over melon rind. Soak all night. Drain and rinse. Cook until tender in clear water.
For 7 lbs. of rind use:
    3 1/2 lbs sugar
    1 pint vinegar
    1 oz. stick cinnamon, 2 ozs. whole cloves,
        1/2 oz. gingerroot (in cheesecloth)
Boil to syrup. Add rind and cook until well flavored.
For 3 mornings bring to boil and pour over pickles.

DILL PICKLES

Hattie Means

Soak cucumbers overnight in cold water.
Pack in jars.
Add sprig of dill.
Cover with boiling brine made of 3 quarts of water,
1 quart of vinegar, 1 cup salt, scant half teaspoon
powdered alum.
Seal hot.

MUTTON EN CASSEROLE

Mrs. Boyd

Brown pieces of mutton stew in butter and let
simmer in the oven. Add carrots, turnips, onions,
tomatoes, chili, cabbage, rice, a little flour and let
cook two hours. Add potatoes last.

STRAWBERRY PRESERVES

Margaret Curtis

Put equal weight sugar and berries together and
bring to a boil. Put out in a quart or two and leave in
sun three days. Cover with glass or cheese cloth.

PERFECTION SALAD

1 envelope Knox gelatine
1/2 cup cold water (Mix 5 minutes)
1 pint boiling water
1 teaspoon salt
1/2 cup mild vinegar
1 cup shredded cabbage
Juice 1 lemon
1/2 cup sugar
2 cups celery
1 can pimento

TAMALE PIE

Daisy Ashley

1 pound hamburger
1 cup white corn meal
6 cups boiling water
1 teaspoon salt in water
1 teaspoon chili powder
1 teaspoon garlic, or 1 medium sized onion
1 medium sized can tomatoes
1 1/2 teaspoon salt

Make mush. Mix 1 1/2 teaspoons salt, chili powder, garlic or onion with meat. Cook until almost dry. Add tomatoes and continue cooking until almost dry. Put half of mush into greased hot pan and then put meat combination on top. Balance of mush on top. Bake 1/2 hour in hot oven.

ROSE BEADS

Gather dark rose petals when flowers are in full bloom. Put them through food chopper several times using large size then next size and at last, fine cutter. After cutting, spread mass in a large rusty iron pan and stir frequently — several times a day. Put through food chopper twice a day for four days. To make beads uniform, use small spoon or thimble. Roll each bead in palms until round and string on slender hat pin. When perfectly dry, rub each one with a soft cloth moistened with almond oil.

Index
